About to cast off with Gavin's powerful RIB ...

ame
ｊuay
feet
ｊf the
came
alongside with his rib, engine ready to go and wheel turned hard over to port while I got the engine on the boat running. Nick Sherman, my companion for the first part of the journey was ready to fend us off if things took a turn for the worst. Gavin was in charge and on the count of three, the guys on the quay pushed off with their feet with all their might, Gavin accelerated to full power and away we roared from the quay! It was not very elegant, but highly effective.

On reflection it was strange starting out from the little quay I had spent so much time on all my life and heading off on an adventure that, with luck and skill, would see me returning here in about three months time, no doubt with many a tale to tell. The crowd had gathered on the quay, munching on the bacon butties, and chatting to each other in loud voices, competing not only with the three piece steel band that had been organised for our send off, but struggling to make themselves heard in the strong wind that seemed to snatch the words out of their mouths.

The day was somewhat surreal, almost like a wedding day, where so much time had been

Final wind recording +/- 30 kts shock horror...

spent planning and everything seemed to be happening all around you and you just kind of floated through it. I can still see, in my mind's eye, the crowd of well-wishers, people chatting around mouthfuls of bacon, watching the band, gripping their coats closer as each gust flapped in, and the Dean looking somewhat wild with white hair and cassock flying in the wind as he watched us leave.

Dean Nicholas told us later that he was about to start the service when he thought he heard someone say "Ehhh... 'e don't half look like Ken Dodd!", which was not the most encouraging comment for him to hear at that stage ...

Off we staggered, and in the end we had to stop waving and just get on with it as Gavin towed us further and further from the dock into even rougher conditions out in the harbour. Once out in the more open water of the channel we were buffeted by the wind and, while the thought of sneaking back to the safety of the quay was appealing, we knew that at some stage we had to head off by ourselves. We thanked Gavin once more and cast off our towline, but ... well ... we weren't going anywhere! At least not in the direction we wanted! We were low in the water and must have looked more like a wallowing whale than a streamlined sailing machine. I hadn't even stowed the dinghy and it was flapping on the forward deck trying to blow away. We really were completely unseaworthy, staggering our way down the channel with too much stuff on board stowed in all the wrong places. I had to shout for Gavin to come back!

So, with Gavin's help alongside again we made progress through the now rolling waves down the harbour. The wind was whipping up the spray and Nick and I took shelter behind the sprayhood, peeping out haphazardly through slitted eyes around the dodger, hoping that

Gavin coming back to give us a hand ...

20

the moment we chose to open our eyes did not coincide with the spray from another wave. We huddled undercover as best we could while poor Gavin was getting absolutely soaked driving the RIB. As we got closer to Hayling Island at the entrance of Chichester Harbour I heard Gavin yell over the noise of the engines "Eh Mike, there's no way you can put to sea in this. You're not going out there!"

We looked ahead and the entrance to Hayling Island was a wall of what looked like huge rolling waves, not helped of course by the fact that when the ebb tide drains out of Chichester Harbour it just goes wild (wind over tide), which was now very much the case. The surf was immense and we had to work out the best plan of action. We crossed in front of the harbour entrance amid rolling waves and reached the safety of Sparkes Marina. The roar of the surf pounding on the sandbanks around the edge of the island was enough to discourage the bravest of mariners. Wow, what an opening leg ... four miles of hell!

"Right guys," I said "Enough! Moor up."

We tied up the boat and went ashore, where the three of us filled ourselves up with hot coffee. Gavin, who was even wetter than us and soaked to the skin, then had to get back in his RIB and make his way up the harbour against the tide back to Bosham.

So, there we were, holed up in Sparkes Marina waiting for the gale to go away ... please!

I turned to Nick after we had seen Gavin off through the rain and said, "I know you've got to go the day after tomorrow, but I get the feeling you're not going to make it to sea. You've gone about as far with me as you're going to go. Four miles! I'm sorry Nick, but I really need to spend some time here and get this boat sorted out."

"Right Mike," he said, "Where do we start?"

And so we set about doing a whole lot of work.

I had to go up on the wharf to sort some things out at the office and left Nick with the new Kedge Anchor, which was still in its box and needed assembling. He opened the box and, as he did, the crown of the anchor shot out of the box and went bonkity-bonk and plop into the water. Many a sailor will know what I mean. Bonkity-bonk and plop are some of the worst sounds any mariner wants to hear and everyone at some stage has experienced the loss of something vital overboard. So when I got back he was looking quite pale. The mud in the marina is a particularly nasty breed of green slime, which swallows up objects and is often reluctant to give them back. The situation wasn't looking too flash.

I have an old saying that I use from time to time, "We are where we are." Things may not be going to plan but we had to deal with what we had and move on. I suggested we wait until the tide had gone out and the boat was sitting on the mud. "I know it's tempting but don't prod around because the piece we're looking for will settle even deeper into the mud. If it's sitting on the top we should be able to see it as it's nice and shiny and we might be able to scoop it up with the net," I explained.

Nick could hardly wait and had the net attached to the end of the boat hook and spent the time, waiting for the tide to drop, practicing his swoop and scoop technique. As soon as the water was low enough he got himself in position over the spot where he thought the piece had landed, had a little feel about, and took a scoop. I think he didn't want to give anything away, but by the look on his face I could tell he'd felt a little bit of extra weight in the net and was hoping it was the piece we needed and not another piece of someone else's long lost junk. He carefully brought it up and we looked in and there was little to see. It looked very dark and muddy as it came towards the surface, but ... there was something in the bottom of the net. Nick reached in and grabbed it with his hand, mud and all. He almost reverently transferred it to safety onboard the boat. It was the piece we were looking for!

Mr Sod at Sea is always there ready to bite you on the bum.

Mr Sod had had his way but it just goes to show that, if you try hard, you can make things turn out for the best – the trick is to give it a damn good go.

What a full on day it had been. By the time we recovered the lost anchor crown, we decided we had had enough stress, tension, adventure and rain for one day and it was time to retire to the local pub for some beer and sustenance. The storm was still blowing and looked like being around for another couple of days, so we knew we should have time to complete most of our tasks before the weather cleared.

Days 2 & 3 – 6ᵀᴴ & 7ᵀᴴ July – Sparkes Marina, Hayling Island

The Monday and Tuesday were spent on final preparations and fitting out the boat. For much of the time, the inside of the boat looked like a giant scran-bag and you could hardly get inside for the kit piled up or stuffed into every available corner. Heavy things all piled on one side, and light stuff like bedding up in the forepeak. No wonder we wallowed so much on the short voyage from Bosham!

A great deal was achieved as we pulled everything off the boat and laid it out, between squalls, well weighted down on the pontoon. We worked piece by piece at stowing items away so that, in theory, not only were they easy to find when needed but kept the boat on an even keel, with weight equally distributed in a sensible manner. We took the time to mount the inflatable Dan Buoy on the stern and make sure it was ready to throw to anyone with the misfortune to find themselves in the briny. The anchor warp and chain were spliced together and marks put along the length to show the water depth when anchoring. We fitted masthead fittings, the solar anchor light and a myriad of other bits and pieces.

It has been pointed out to me that this stuff should, perhaps, have been done before we left Bosham as the two days spent in Sparkes Marina getting everything done weren't in the itinerary.

But the Lord works in mysterious ways and, because of the storm, we were given the time to get almost everything ship shape. The storm was perhaps a blessing in disguise!

Nick was a real trooper and, with his help, I was ready to head for sea by the evening of the seventh, when he headed home, having endured a day where we covered four miles under tow and two days stormbound in a little boat bumping up and down in the marina at Hayling Island.

The Bosham Sailing Club Burgee

Farewell and Adieu

CHAPTER 4 – AND SO TO SEA …

"Dear God, Be good to me. My boat is so small and the sea is so wide."

The Breton Fisherman's Prayer

DAY 4 – 8TH JULY – HAYLING ISLAND TO YARMOUTH

My new, but tried and true crewmember, Dick Pratt, arrived at the marina on the morning of the eighth. The wind had dropped and swung to the southwest and the sea state, while lumpy, looked manageable for a pair of seasoned mariners. Dick had accompanied me on several previous delivery voyages across the English Channel, we knew each other well and had a mass of sea miles under our belts.

Our first port of call, after the two day sojourn at Hayling Island waiting for the storm to pass, was Yarmouth on the Isle of Wight. We had to beat down the western Solent into the typical short chop that, luckily as it turned out, *Theo's Future* rode remarkably well. Getting out round Hayling Island had used a lot more fuel than I had anticipated and, by the time we had made our way westward along the south coast, sailed the Solent between the mainland and the Isle of Wight and neared our destination, we were perilously low on petrol and darkness had already fallen. The seemingly huge Yarmouth – Lymington ferry was leaving the dock as we arrived and we rather nervously edged our way in against the strong ebb current, hoping and praying that the meagre remains in the bottom of the tank would suffice … much to our relief they did and we coasted up to the fuel dock on vapours.

The harbour master gave us a very warm welcome and waived the port fee, which was a generous gesture I was to experience in all but a few of the ports I visited. His night watchman reopened the fuel point to serve us petrol and we made enquiries about food and liquid refreshments. As it turned out, we had arrived too late for food in the pub but the landlady of a certain establishment, enjoying her late night cigarette, took pity on us – two soggy dishevelled creatures from the deep. She let us in and poured us a pint. Needless to say, it barely touched the sides!

When we got back to the marina, the staff were incredibly generous and shared their rations of sandwiches and crisps with us. This earned them Fight for Sight T-shirts and pens … how kind they were!

Day 5 – 9th July – Yarmouth to Poole

Next morning we were up at 5am and left the relatively quiet waters of Yarmouth for a very wild ride indeed. The wind was building from the southwest and we were soon in the thick of some of the worst conditions I was to experience in the entire trip. Dick is a windsurfer, one of the top 20 surfboarders in England in fact, so quite at home in the surf and swells, but even he would admit that this was really too much.

We grimly made our way out of the relative shelter of the Solent, down past the perilous Shingles Bank and out beyond the beautiful but rugged Needles. These sentinels have stood guard over this part of England's coast for centuries and, no doubt, been the witness to many a foolish sailor, who presses on with his voyage when all the signs say stop, change course, bear away to safer waters. The standing waves out there were awesome and somewhat terrifying as they relentlessly tossed us up and over again and again and again. The halyards slapped in a disjointed fashion, seemingly joining with the screaming and wailing from the rigging as we were buffeted from front to back and side to side. If a vessel can express its agony, the torture of the twist and toss, *Theo's Future* was letting us know in a loud and unignorable cacophony that she was not enjoying the experience. To make matters worse, the anchor and chain worked their way loose from where they had been stowed quickly, but not very securely, at the bow of the boat and, with a low pitched jangle of heavy metal, slid over the side. While we were quick to gather them back up, it was not easy in the rough conditions and the anchor made several nasty dings in the hull before we got it back on board and securely tied down again. We had planned to head for Weymouth to stop for the night and, on an ordinary day, this would have been quite feasible. Today, however, was no ordinary day!

Heavy weather sailing ... past the Shingle Bank

When you're at sea you can't say, "Well, I've written a plan so that's what we're going to do." You have to say, "Well I've written a plan but the weather is this, the tide is that, the conditions are the other, so we've got to adapt the plan to survive the day and have another go tomorrow rather than push on, on a fools errand, and risk everything."

The plan in this case pretty much went out the window.

Is there anyway through the maelstrom?

Both Dick and I were using up vast amounts of energy as we worked to keep the boat balanced in the huge swells, making sure that we hit each wave at just the right angle so the water washed over us, down the deck and away. It would not take much to see us broach or roll on our side, as the waters twisted and turned us to their will, and while we had washboards in to keep the interior dry, it would not take much to swamp our little vessel.

We changed our plan and altered course. The boat seemed happiest pointing across Christchurch Bay towards Poole Harbour, which seemed as good a place as any to head for. While the waves continued to batter us with walls of green water and eye stinging salty spray, we were able to make some headway.

That day was a slogging sail I will never forget. Progress was slow, 3 knots at best. Hours seemed to dissolve into each other as we endured the ongoing onslaught and wildness of mother nature. Days like that are absolutely no fun!

Luckily for us, my good friends Caroline and Tim Harding, who are the parents of my son Simon's girlfriend Miranda, lived near our new destination. Before the voyage they had expressed disappointment that we were going to bypass Poole on our way around the country.

I'd told Caroline, "I'm sorry, but Poole is just too far off the beaten track."

"Oh," she'd said, "We'd love to see you."

"No, I'm sorry, it's far too much of a detour and well out of our way."

Well, by now I was more than prepared to eat humble pie. A friendly face at the end of such a day does much to revive the spirits and I hoped to contact her once we had reached more sheltered waters, provided my phone had survived its dousing.

At last, as we got closer to shore and in the lee of land, the waves began to regain a semblance of order after their unruly tantrum and we were able to catch our breath and relax our tensioned muscles. Watching the huge Brittany ferry negotiate the treacherous sandbanks on either side of the entrance to Poole Harbour reminded us, though, that we were still on duty. We raised the centre plate and eased our way into the smaller shallow inside channel, which runs at right angles along the sea wall. It is not unusual to see five knots of tide round the narrow entrance and, once through the racing tide, we breathed a huge sigh of relief when at last our lines were safely attached to the quayside. We were in, soaked, but we were in, so we were happy. Within minutes we were hailed from another boat, and invited to drink post wedding Beaujolais with some old Sapper friends from the Royal Engineer Yacht Club, Mark and Alison Tilley, who had abandoned their attempt to reach Cherbourg in their Bavaria 38, which was, by comparison, significantly more boat than our little vessel.

I had given Caroline a ring when we arrived, and said, "You'll never guess where we are."

"Are you in my harbour?" she said.

"If Poole's your harbour, then, yes, we're here, and what's more we're soaking wet."

"Right," she said, "We'll be down at five o'clock, and you're coming back to the farm."

In the meantime, I phoned home to talk to Pip and fill her in on our progress (or lack thereof). This is when we realised how useful the tracking system was as, when I rang and said, "We're in Poole Harbour," she said, "Yes, I know. I can see you on the town quay – third boat out!" Amazingly, she was able to zoom right in using Google Earth on the Internet. Gosh, I thought, I'd better make sure I kept my trousers on! I later realised she couldn't actually see the boat, but rather a red boat shape that represented where we were, so didn't have to worry about scandalous photos appearing in the national news.

Caroline and Tim turned up at the appointed hour and we were delighted to see them, when they arrived at the dockside. They whipped Dick and me away to their lovely Dorset farmhouse and offered us a bath or shower. I opted for the bath and went into the bathroom to be faced with a huge old, deep, hot steaming bath, complete with bubbles. I could hardly believe my eyes, it looked so inviting. I could feel myself dozing off just looking at it and, sure enough, I slid beneath the bubbles and fell soundly asleep. I was awoken some time later by a tremendous thumping at the bathroom door and Dick calling, "Come on Mike. Are you coming to the pub for supper?"

Well, by then the water had got quite cold so it was time to make a move. I was out and dressed within minutes. Off we went for a scrummy supper at the Anchor Pub near the River Stour. Caroline offered us real beds that night but, though sorely tempted, we were staunch and went back to the soggy boat as we had to be up at five the next morning to be ready to catch the tide. We regretted our decision more intensely when the stench of our wet and water-soaked gear greeted our nostrils as we took out the washboards upon our return.

Sleeping in the forepeak was out of the question as we had discovered a design fault with the boat that was to plague us for several days of our voyage until we found someone to make the changes needed. The anchor well at the front of the boat has two little drain holes feeding two hoses that, in theory, fed any excess water to the outside of the hull. In practice, however, the boat had home-made fittings that didn't fit together well and were not watertight. In heavy seas the anchor well was almost constantly filled with water, which found its way down into the cabin.

Water is a sneaky creature that streams through the tiniest holes, quietly delivering what appears to be bucket loads within minutes. As a result, the forward bunk and anything on it was continually sodden. So, with much lamenting for warm beds in a Dorset farmhouse, we spent the night as best we could in the quarter berths.

CHAPTER 5 – WARNING SHOTS OVER THE BOW ...

DAY 6 – 10TH JULY – POOLE TO WEYMOUTH

We were woken by a voice from the dockside ...

"Oy! You said you'd be up and about at five o'clock, and here you are fast asleep. I've been up for three hours doing your washing."

Caroline (God Bless Her) had appeared with our washing, which was clean and, more importantly, dry. It was six in the morning and we had slept in! It didn't take long though to get ready and after a hearty breakfast of Brookie's porridge we departed for Weymouth for the second time, much refreshed and on a high (both in spirits and tide).

Out we sailed, past Old Harry, which is a rather precarious rock stack, now at threat from erosion as the sea wears away the base of the rocks. Originally carved out from the chalk cliffs by the sea the rocks have stood for hundreds of years and are thought to be named after Harry Payne, a local pirate who stashed his loot nearby. Further south we went round the corner past the lighthouse at Anvil Point to be met by big rolling seas along the south facing coast. The headland there has a shelf that sticks out below the water level and, when you have the tide running one way and the wind the other, it creates standing waves, which are even worse where currents meet. Today, this was a very dangerous area indeed and we fought hard to get across as quickly as possible, keen to put yet another tumultuous experience behind us. Only day six and I was beginning to wonder if I was ever to have a truly pleasant day of sailing. The rain had not left me alone for a day and the wind refused to cooperate. Already I could feel the tendrils of exhaustion taxing my reserves, as, not only was this turning out to be a physical test, but my mind was constantly busy dealing with tides, weather, courses, winds, equipment, what to eat, where to go ...

We were just about to emerge from the other side of the wash when we were pounced upon by the crew of the Bovington Tank Firing Range safety RIB, who politely, but firmly requested that we tack away to the south to avoid the firing range danger area.

What? And go back into that ... no way!

I advised him that this was not possible in such a small boat and I replied on Channel 8 that he was basically asking us to endanger ourselves by rejoining the tidal race and going back to the conditions from which we had just escaped. No thanks!

I was within my rights to sail through the area. The safety vessel could only issue an advisory to go round, they could not say we must change course.

Bear in mind I understand the need for practice, which the gunners have to do if they're going to biff the Taliban on the nose or whoever it is that we're fighting.

"Train Hard and Fight Easy!" is after all, the military way.

I explained to the crew of the safety vessel, who were all ex warrant officers, that as an ex-soldier I understood the need for practice and was not deliberately trying to piss them off, but in this case I must insist that I carry on with my course.

At sea, as the captain of the vessel, you alone must make the decisions about what is safe or not. In this situation the safety of my tiny boat was far more important than Gunner Smith in a tank firing an extra round before NAAFI break.

Well, there wasn't a lot they could do, and after some interesting discussion with those on land, firing eventually ceased with a change in the firing plan for the day so we could sail through. Bizarre, but true. I certainly didn't want to take a tank shell through the mainsail!

We set course for Lulworth Cove, where Dick hadn't been before, to have a break from the rough conditions. This fabulous little circular cove is where the real 'Lawrence of Arabia' retired. Made famous in a film by the same name, he was an intelligence officer who worked for the British in the Middle East and galvanized the Arabs to run their own countries. He became much revered by the Arabs, but less popular with the allied forces when he refused to take advantage of his relationship to benefit the political aims of the outside countries. Needless to say, his services were no longer required and he chose this rather secluded little spot to live after leaving His Majesty's service.

We sailed carefully through the narrow entrance to the cove and picked up a mooring close to shore in the lee of the surrounding cliffs so we could relax for a few moments over a well deserved cup of tea and a feed. Blow me down, but the firing range safety RIB also came in for a break from the weather too. They seemed cheerful enough and gave us a wave so, luckily, there were no hard feelings!

Restored in spirit and energy, we headed out again an hour later and completed the day's sailing to Weymouth as planned. We were behind schedule and the tide was against us now, but we were in the shelter of Portland Bill so it didn't matter so much. We got to Weymouth Harbour at six o'clock and moored up for the night. Dick's time with me was over, so he packed his things and, with some relief no doubt to be on dry, solid land, departed for normal life.

Lieutenant Colonel Pat Clarke is an old friend and fellow Sapper from the Royal Engineers who joined me for the next leg of the voyage. I knew he was coming, but one minute I was alone and the next he was there. It was as if he appeared out of nowhere, and what a delight it was to see him. We have sailed and raced boats together for more than 30 years and his appearance at the Weymouth Town Quay lifted my somewhat sagging morale. With Pat around, I knew that I could tackle Portland Bill with renewed confidence. He dumped his bag and declared, "Right, let's go to the pub!" Another old friend from the sappers, Colonel Michael Gill MBE who is a past Commodore of the Royal Dorset Yacht Club, joined us at the pub for cheeky beers and a chat. It was a relatively early night as we had to be up early to catch the tide, and with the treacherous Portland Bill to negotiate, neither Pat nor I wanted to be the worse for wear.

DAY 7 – 11TH JULY – WEYMOUTH TO BRIXHAM

We were up at 5 am, aiming for a slack water rounding of Portland Bill, using the inside channel. You have two choices going round the Bill, either right outside the wild waters known as 'The Shambles' and the tidal race which means sailing seven or eight miles offshore or you hug the coast. I mean really 'hug the coast', only a few feet off land using the inside channel. The inside channel is obviously not a goer in stormy conditions. Even on a fine day it's dangerous enough, especially when the numerous lobster pots increase the chances of wrapping your prop, which is the last thing you want, and yet you need to keep the engine running to provide a bit of extra oomph.

We had timed our run to perfection, arriving at Portland Bill just ahead of slack tide. We positioned ourselves to take advantage of the change in the tide and had a speedy but incident free ride as we were swooshed around the headland by the outgoing water and pushed out into Lyme Bay.

Yes, once again the wind was – you guessed it – on da nose! The wind built and turned slightly to the south so we were forced to put two reefs in the mainsail, lessening the sail area and making it easier for us to control the boat so we weren't blown over by the gusts. We also kept the engine going to help us make way and speed up our passage. With the wind blowing from the southeast the sea swell also increased with plenty of large green waves or 'greenies' coming to have a look at us, making our life even wetter. Lyme Bay seemed to go on for ever and the wind was still not being particularly kind to us as it continued to swing against our favour and we ended pointing, not towards our destination of Brixham, but towards Exmouth, which, despite having the Royal Marines Commando Training Centre at nearby Lympstone and where I was an instructor from 1970-72, was not really where we wanted to go.

Once again, we amended our plan and, seeing nature seemed intent on taking us towards Exmouth, that's where we decided to go. Not much choice really… been there, done that … tried to get to Weymouth, ended up in Poole; tried to get to Brixham, ended up in Exmouth.

And then 'IT' happened …

Horrors …

The engine stopped!

It just stopped. We checked the fuel, checked the hoses, checked everything. We simply couldn't restart it and I can remember tearing the skin between my fingers from trying to restart it again and again and again. This was serious stuff!

One might ask, 'Why?'

Yes, we were in a yacht with sails but we were in a very small yacht and, with the weather conditions deteriorating, the last thing we wanted was to be without power. Little boats do not like big seas and big winds and, to tell you the truth, the people on board like them even less!

Sometimes, when things can't be changed, you just have to harden up and get on with it … so, we sailed.

The wind, as if knowing we were without any other form of propulsion but our sails, decided to play with us and dropped away … so we floated.

With the dropping of the wind, conditions on board became more pleasant and, while floating along, my mind turned to consider where we should go to get the engine fixed. I wasn't sure what was wrong with it and I wasn't sure if there would be a Yamaha agent or repairer in Exmouth.

What were we to do? It was Friday afternoon, we were miles from land and, once we finally made it to shore, the chances of finding someone to do repairs over the weekend were slim at best.

As if by magic my prayers and muttered thoughts were answered and, amazingly, the breeze suddenly came in from the North West and, after a gentle nudge from Pat along the lines of "No Brookie, you can't drink beer with your old Royal Marine mates today … ", we put up every ounce of sailcloth we could find and flew before the breeze straight towards Brixham, the first time we had been 'off the wind' and under full plain sail in the whole voyage!

The thing about sailing is that it's always easiest to go where the wind is blowing you.

When we reached Brixham, just like the sailors of old with their Brixham Trawlers, we tacked around the sea wall into the harbour, turned up into the wind to stop the boat and dropped the anchor. I called Neil, the harbour master, who had been expecting us, and he came out in his launch and towed us in. We made fast for the night in the very spot we were supposed to after all. Who'd have thought!

Even though it was so late, Judi Hedger, who is my daughter-in-law Jayne's mother met us there, along with her second daughter Claire, Claire's partner Simon and their two daughters, Georgia and Olivia. Despite it nearly being the middle of the night, Claire kindly collected our filthy clothes, also taking with her my phone, which had been submerged during the course of the day. Simon seemed to think he could get it working, and at this stage I was willing to try anything. She returned the whole lot the next morning, clothes clean, dry and neatly folded, and also with my phone, which seemed to have miraculously recovered after spending the night in her Aga to dry out!

We had dinner the evening we arrived with Judi and even popped a bottle of champers to celebrate … well … life really! I kept the cork and later, back on the boat, used it to solve one of our leakage problems. I cut the cork to fit the drain holes in the cockpit combing at the side of the main hatch, which worked fine when the boat was upright but, when heeled over and awash with green water, meant that the water draining off the hatch ran down the sides and poured into the cabin below.

DAY 8 – 12ᵀᴴ JULY - BRIXHAM TO DARTMOUTH

Judi became our saviour and driver in Brixham, delivering us across the hill next morning to Kingswear, near the mouth of the river Dart, and to the only Yamaha Agent for miles, just as he was locking up on the Saturday morning.

"Ooh, stop," I called out to him with a note of desperation in my voice, "please wait, I need your help!"

I went through what had happened and also pointed out that the engine wasn't mine but was owned by Yamaha UK and had been lent to me for the expedition.

I told him I was pretty sure that water had got into the fuel and the system would be right as rain once it was flushed through. I must have grovelled quite convincingly as he agreed to reopen the shop and told us to come back at one o'clock. The relief in my heart, phew!

"Right," said Judi, "I'm taking you for the best and biggest breakfast you can possibly imagine."

We left the car in Kingswear and went across the River Dart on the little chain ferry to Dartmouth where we found an amazing breakfast place, which served us gallons of fresh orange juice and huge plates overflowing with fabulous grub. The view back to Kingswear was charming, with rows of brightly coloured houses built into the cliffs and natural contours of the hills. For once the sun was shining and we had a great catch up before returning to pick up the engine, which had suffered exactly as I thought. The petrol tank lies in a locker on one side of the boat in the cockpit. When heeled over, the locker becomes flooded with some of the water from the cockpit drain and the seawater had got into the breather hose of the petrol tank, ruining the fuel.

It was going to be awkward to change the position of the fuel tank but I managed to solve the problem by getting an extra tank for the other side and shutting the appropriate breather valve as I tacked. This has proved to be effective and, thus far, has prevented the problem from recurring.

Chris Hoyle, the mechanic, was very kind and presented me with a small spares pack to take with me for the rest of my journey. I made sure he put one of his 'Hoyle Marine' stickers onto the engine to remind me of his generous contribution, which ensured I could continue my voyage.

We headed back to Brixham, where Pat and I got everything out of the boat and laid it on the wharf to try and dry it out in the afternoon sun. We had a little time to spare as we were waiting for a third crewmember to join us and wouldn't depart Brixham until later in the day for the short hop to Dartmouth.

While in Brixham I had another brainwave, which doesn't happen very often! Children had been coming down to the boat to have a look and ask questions about the brightly coloured flags and stickers. I had the idea of creating a lucky dip bag filled with RNLI goodies for the kids. It was, after all, about helping kids and I find that children are always open to helping other children if you explain what you are doing and why. The lucky dip bag went on to be a great hit and proved to be a fabulous tool for raising money.

Time and again at various ports around the coast I was to meet children at the dockside who were interested in the stickers and flags displayed on *Theo's Future*. I would tell them about my voyage and ask if they'd like to take part in the adventure by having a dip in the lucky dip bag and answering a question. Of course they would! They'd put a hand into the lucky dip lifeboat bag and drag out a teddy bear on a keyring.

"Can I really keep this?" they'd say.

"Yes, if you can answer a question about the lifeboat."

Oh no ... they're under exam conditions now ...

"What is a lifeboat?" I ask them

"Oooh ... it's orange and blue," they'd say.

"Yes, but what does it do?"

"Well ... it goes and saves people."

"Yes! Well done, you can keep the keyring."

Off they trot with their prize and the first people they tell are their mum and dad who get dragged along to see what they're talking about. They see the little boat with all the banners and fun going on, ask what it's all about, and usually make a donation.

So, without being overly commercial, for a net outlay of £3.50 to buy the teddy bear keyring, we usually receive a twenty pound note from the parents. £16.50 to the charity ... Thank you very much!

CHAPTER 6 – RUMBLE IN THE JUNGLE …

"When you're sailing, you're living … Everything else is just waiting!"

Anon

Jilly Rumble arrived to a dockside piled with all sorts of paraphernalia and, as someone new to a boat, she must have wondered how so much stuff had come out of such a small vessel. I could not help but take the opportunity to proudly introduce her to my as yet unused, but ready for action, pride and joy – the Porta-Potti, displayed majestically like a throne on the dock of the marina, and bought especially for the occasion to cater for some of my more genteel crewmembers, when needs must. Jilly looked a little horrified at the pile, the Porta-Potti and the two rather rugged men she was to share the boat with for the next few days. I don't think first impressions got a lot better when she realised just how much room, or lack thereof, was inside the boat. Bear in mind we were still trying to work out where the leak up front was coming from and, as this area was to be her domain, she was faced with a very small, triangular, damp area in which to make herself at home.

What a trooper she was!

The forepeak was quickly assembled into a semblance of order and privacy, becoming a ladies boudoir, complete with a sort of harem curtain. The gear was stowed in all the correct places, and the Porta-Potti was positioned in pride of place ready for her ladyship. Jilly, it turned out later, admitted to an almost paranoid fear of the contraption and was most relieved to find that there was a vital piece missing and it couldn't be used. The bucket and chuckit method would have to suffice.

Drying out everything in Brixham Marina

Jilly worked for Fight for Sight and had taken time off away from the office to accompany me and find out, first hand, what was involved in my fundraising mission. She had never sailed before and already she was grappling with the sheer practicalities, before even putting to sea. Talk about a steep learning curve and being thrown in the deep end!

I'm amazed she didn't run screaming from the dock as there is a huge difference between a lovely cosy office job working for Fight for Sight, to cabin boy aboard the good ship *Theo's Future* with not much room for dignity, or anything else for that matter.

Jilly, however, is made of stern stuff, and quickly adapted to life onboard, even creating her own hamster nest in the forepeak. Yes, it was still wet, so perhaps it was more of an aquatic type of hamster. On her first morning aboard she emerged from her nest and gave a very life-like impression of a hamster preening, something she was to continue each morning as part of her onboard ritual.

Despite having never sailed before, she took to the sea like a duck to water. Pat took her under his wing and we motored her out for some basic sail training and experience. By later that afternoon she was at the helm as we motor sailed out of Brixham Harbour. You could tell by the look on her face that she was hooked when we turned off the motor and all that could be heard was the sound of the breeze in our sails.

The conditions were so perfect we even popped up the furling gennaker in Royal Marine Colours;

"Blue for the sea that we go across in our landing craft, Yellow for the beaches up which we assault, Green for the fields where the enemy objective lies, and Red ... for the red light district in the town behind!"

The boat speed picked up and Jilly said she was having fun but I did notice a slight whitening of the knuckles and a much tighter grip on the tiller. The wind swung round ninety degrees and headed us, so we had to swiftly roll in or furl the gennaker, using the Karver continuous line furling system that I insisted was installed when setting up the boat. It was originally designed for single-handed sailors in the Mini Transat Yacht Race and I have become a confirmed convert. Rather than having two sheets or ropes attached, the sheet is one continuous piece and makes handling of the headsail safer and easier in all conditions, especially when there are few crew on board.

Yes – all facilities provided

Shit! Sat on them

A welcome cuppa …

Jilly "Rumble in the Jungle" sailing lesson No. 1

Lesson 1 complete – smiles all round

West Country Dawn

We made our way around the Froward Point headland and, as the evening drew on, we rounded the south cardinal mark, a buoy that marked the entrance to the River Dart, and moored alongside another yacht at the Dartmouth town quay.

We had supper in the Cherub Pub, one of the oldest pubs in the West Country, built in about 1380. It's so old and rickety you have to walk up the stairs on an angle because

Pat Clarke (sailing instructor extraordinaire!) with Jilly Rumble

the whole place is on such a lean. Nothing like a good sail to build your appetite for a satisfying pint and a good big plate of pub grub!

DAY 9 – 13ᵀᴴ JULY – DARTMOUTH TO SALCOMBE

Simon, Claire, Georgia and Olivia, together with their dear friend Teresa plus her son Jay, met us again in Dartmouth the next morning and came aboard for a wee trip up the river for a banyan – a trip on a boat for a picnic. Claire had never been on a boat before and enjoyed her short adventure; all the young had a go at steering and it was a lovely jaunt in the morning sunshine.

Claire is self-employed and, through one of her contacts, gained sponsorship for *Theo's Future* from an American company, which supplied the paint for the centre plate, along with a very generous donation of one thousand dollars, which, due to events later in the saga, which you will now have to continue reading in order to find out, was not forthcoming.

After lunch, we dropped them back at Dartmouth, said goodbye and motored out of the River Dart, round Start Point and across the bay towards Salcombe. It was quite a short leg, but ideal as an introduction to sailing for Jilly. The day was sparkling and we had a fabulous incident free trip, going right into the Salcombe-Kingsbridge estuary, where we had a fabulous welcome from the Salcombe Island Cruising Club. Based on an old Mersey Ferry, *Egremont*, the ship is used as a sail-training base and is fully set up with accommodation and catering facilities.

We were invited to moor up alongside and show *Theo's Future* to the kids at the sailing school. The club was extremely generous and we made use of their piping hot showers and had a few ciders before going ashore for a wonderful feed of the local scallops in the King's Head pub.

Donations were handed in to us later, when we paused on our way back to the boat for a drink in the ship's bar. It may not seem that we were doing much fund raising in the evening, but the lucky dip bag was dragging in plenty of cash from parents along the way.

"We are, I'm afraid, employing children to get mum and dad to cough up the house keeping!" I explained to someone at one point.

Andy and July Skentelbery, Cornish Trans Atlantic buddies …

With my niece Jane and her son Freddie in Plymouth

DAY 10 – 14TH JULY – SALCOMBE TO PLYMOUTH TO FALMOUTH

The next day we were up at the crack of dawn as we had a long day planned, heading for Falmouth in Cornwall with a stop at Plymouth on the way to see my niece Janey, her son Freddie, and to do an interview with one of the local papers, *The Plymouth Herald.*

We were off by five o'clock, motoring out in the dark, carefully looking out for moorings that might get snagged on our way out of the estuary. We sailed across Bigbury Bay and round the Great Mewstone, a great triangular shaped rock that juts out of the sea as if shoved skyward from beneath the water. Into Plymouth Sound we sailed, once again through a firing range danger zone but, fortunately on a day when the guns were silent. We tied up at Queen Anne's Battery Marina and met up with Janey and her son Freddie who had come to meet us. We had to wait around for the press to turn up as they were running late and this, unfortunately, ate into our sailing time. By the time we left Plymouth, we were nearly an hour behind schedule, which may not seem like much but, when relying on the tide to assist us along the way, can make a serious difference to the amount of ground, or, in this case, sea we can cover.

The wind was rising as we departed Plymouth via the western entrance. We had to motor sail against the incoming swell of the waves across Whitesand Bay, with the wind ... yes, you guessed it ... on da nose! These conditions make for a wet and tiring ride at the best of times as the boat rises up the face of the wave and drops down on the other side with a groaning shudder as the rigging is jolted back and forth. With each landing the spray flies and the seawater rushes down the deck, swirling into every corner it can find before escaping overboard to its more familiar environment. Anything not tied down is tossed haphazardly with the movement of the boat and, as is often the case on a day such as this, we were all very keen to reach shelter.

The simple logistics of three adults on board a small boat meant for great innovation and a lot of compromise on the part of each crewmember at times. Moving round inside the boat consisted of working out where to put your feet, especially as you took the first most important step from the cockpit into the cabin. There was an art to ensuring your foothold was firm enough to hold you if the boat moved suddenly, and to complicate matters you also had to ensure your feet didn't squash some vital piece of equipment or food as you moved around.

Another problem with living aboard a sailing boat is that an object stored somewhere at the start of the day, is not necessarily in the same place at the end of the day. As the boat heels over, objects tend to tip and roll around and the most common place for finding some things is on the floor or in the bilge, hence the need to find a space to land your foot without squashing or breaking something.

While everything had initially been stored securely, tools, instruments and equipment are used on a regular basis. They are not however, always returned to their original home, and as a result the days were constantly punctuated with: 'Have you seen ... ?'; 'Do you know where the ... ?'; 'Who's got the ... ?'

Dave Proud RNLI Falmouth Station mechanic

By the time we got to Falmouth we were tired, wet and hungry, and the boat interior looked like someone had shaken everything loose, with all sorts of bits and pieces thrown helter-skelter around inside the cabin.

Luckily Stephanie, Pat Clarke's wife, met us at Falmouth and welcomed us back to their home for hot showers and grub. Jilly left us the next day, complete with bruises, an addiction for sailing and lots of new knowledge and priceless experiences.

She left me a note;

*"Well Mike, You are right. My life will never be the same. Some people go on holiday and catch Malaria, or Typhoid, but I've caught the sailing bug! You've given me a fantastic experience, and I have learnt so much from you and Patrick; how to tie knots … how to feel the wind … and how to get a gloomy press photographer to take your photo, and smile. Before I came away, some (lots of) people told me I was brave, and I didn't totally understand because I was ignorant of what was involved. I thought I could have a few days away, and top up my tan! I had a few surprises, and discovered what you were really talking about, and my respect for you has increased one hundred fold. You are one of life's heroes, and although I am sure it helps that you are also stark raving mad, I have every confidence that you will succeed in helping thousands of children with LCA. I may not be up in the Hamster's nest at the front, but I am with you in spirit. I wish you jolly sailing and lots of love,
Jilly Rumble – Rumble in the Jungle x"*

Lovely!

DAY 11 – 15ᵗʰ JULY – FALMOUTH

I ended up staying two nights with Pat and Stephanie. We had a huge fundraising evening at the Royal Cornwall Yacht Club organised by Andrew Poole. Amongst

With Pat Clarke and Jilly Rumnble – A Happy Crew.

other fundraising activities, we had a raffle so I was faced with getting some prizes. One of the prizes was to be a weekend at Benbow B & B. Pip had told me I could only offer this as a prize three times during my voyage around the country, so one down, two to go. We got wine from the local supermarket and Pat fixed a family ticket to the Maritime Museum in Falmouth, a round of golf at the local golf course and quite a few other nice bits and pieces. We sold raffle tickets and I did my little talk with my pop-up stand. That evening the club was full of working boat skippers who had come in after the evening race and, being experienced gaff sailors, they were full of how I could improve the halyard system on my little Cape Cutter and had numerous useful tips and hints, some of which I have since put to good use.

The club was also full of pilots and helicopter crews from the Royal Naval Air Station Culdrose, and they said "We know you're going to be at sea tomorrow heading down towards Penzance. You might be in for a surprise!"

Uh oh, they were going to buzz us!

I know they need to be constantly training, after all they have to be able to find boats at sea and perform rescues, but I wasn't sure that I wanted to be their practice dummy.

Sounds exciting doesn't it, but when you're in a tiny boat on a big sea and a dirty great helicopter starts buzzing you at low altitude, it isn't really much fun, as the boat rocks like crazy and you have to hang on!

CHAPTER 7 – ROUND THE BOTTOM ...

DAY 12 – 16ᵀᴴ JULY – FALMOUTH TO PENZANCE

Pat continued on with me the next day as we carried on with our voyage towards Penzance. At nine o'clock that morning we had a photo shoot, with photos taken from a RIB of *Theo's Future* flying her new Cayman Islands gennaker, complete with Sir Turtle, the peg leg pirate. The rugged Cornish coast is famous for its stories of smugglers, pirates and shipwrecks, so what an appropriate image to fly! As I had no crew, Pat suggested that I take Imke Wels, a German teacher, who was staying with them. She jumped at the opportunity and we had a lovely time cruising around the harbour under full sail. The Cayman Islands High Commission had kindly sponsored the gennaker together with a healthy donation to the kitty. And then disaster ... she bent forward, snagged the emergency toggle and accidentally triggered the auto-inflate switch on her life-jacket. *"No worries"* I exclaimed, hardly able to conceal my smile. It filled up so full that she could barely get it off on reaching the dock – bad luck but no surprises to find Mr Sod is alive and well in Falmouth too! She was so embarrassed and a touch cross with herself too which was absolutely unnecessary.

By ten o'clock, we were heading out of Falmouth, south across Falmouth Bay and down the coast past the Manacles. Made up of three nasty groups of rocks,

Gennaker "up and away"   *Farewell Falmouth ...*

many of which are submerged, or can only be seen at low tide, the Manacles lie off a headland that protrudes into the English Channel, just south of Porthoustock, and, as such, is in the direct path of anyone wanting to take the fastest route round the bottom of the country. As you can well imagine, they have claimed many ships over the years and are now a popular dive spot because of the number of shipwrecks that lie below the surface. Fortunately, the rocks are now well known, with a cardinal mark to remind you to keep clear. You don't go near the Manacles and certainly not between the Manacles and land unless you're a local fisherman and know the waters very well.

We carried on and rounded the Lizard, the most southern point of Britain, with its own collection of rugged rocks that, like the Manacles, have captured many an unsuspecting sailor over the centuries. Now with its own lighthouse to warn off visitors from the sea, the peninsula is popular with tourists. We must have been about two miles further to the west when suddenly there was the roar of a helicopter; only one helicopter, but a large Sea King Air Sea

Where's the Lizard!

Imke Wels Michelin Girl ...

Buzzed by the Royal Navy ...

Rescue chopper, which came screaming in and banked right over the top of us! It sent us rocking all over the place. We were hanging on for grim death, with waves washing across the deck, the mast creaking, spray flying and the sound of items bouncing around inside the boat. Lots of banter and cheeky messages, their present to me to acknowledge what we were doing, and of course, great practice for them, as it was a training flight. All perfectly safe I'm sure, in aeronautical terms, and an awful lot of fun. In nautical terms, however, we may have described it as something quite different and that can't be printed!

Fortunately, they didn't stay to play for long so, once they'd departed and the sea state calmed, we took a few minutes to sort ourselves out and carried on across Mounts Bay, where we anchored at St Michael's Mount, one of Cornwall's most famous landmarks, rowing ashore for a quick look before continuing on our way. Fabled to have been the home of a giant called Cormoran, the hill which sits just off the coast is connected to the mainland by a causeway which can be crossed at low tide. Over the centuries the hill has had many uses. It was the guardian for a thriving port from where tin was exported for many years until, it is said, a vision of the Archangel of St Michael appeared on the Mount in 495 AD, whence it gained its name and, as a result, became a holy place. It was the site of a 14th century Benedictine Abbey, a fortress during the Wars of the Roses and the English Civil War, and is said to be the first hill upon which a beacon was lit to warn the English of the Spanish Armada. There was obviously lots to see!

We didn't stop long, however, and sailed on, reaching Penzance at four o'clock, where we just missed getting access to the inner harbour, via the lock, so instead tied up in the outer harbour. This proved to be the better option the next morning as we could leave when we wanted and were not restricted by the lock-opening timetable.

That evening Claire Hall arrived. We had last seen her and her family at Dartmouth. When her partner Simon, who was supposed to be crew, was unable to join us, Claire stepped up. "This family is not going to let Mike down, so I'm going," she declared!

Considering the trip up the river Dart for a banyan was her only boating experience so far, she had no kit, had never been to sea and was about to sail around Land's End, one of Britain's most notorious coastlines, she was very brave. (Naïve definitely, but very brave!)

46

Claire Hall, first time in a sailing boat.

Nervous smile whilst clenching the tiller.

Yes I can do this.

That night Pat, Claire and I had a veritable feast in what I would consider to be one of the best coastal pubs in England, called the Admiral Benbow. It wasn't just the name that attracted me for, while it doesn't look like much from the outside, inside they've reassembled parts of a Nelsonian frigate that had been brought up from the seabed by divers and reconstructed it in the pub. When you sit at the captain's table, you may well be sitting where the real captain sat to entertain his officers. It is incredible! Add to that the local fresh fish from Newlyn, the adjacent fishing harbour, and the experience is fantastic.

DAY 13 – 17ᵀᴴ JULY - PENZANCE TO ST IVES

Next morning we slipped away from the outer harbour wall at six o'clock, under engine, and motored past the walled fishing port of Newlyn, which, while only minutes away, has its very own community and character. Strange though it may seem, as they both share the sea, fishermen and sailors do not mix well and usually keep to themselves. At eight o'clock, we began to pick up the westerly current around Land's End as Longships Light and its jagged rocks came into view.

The Longships Lighthouse stands on Carn Bras, the highest of three rocks, which rises 12 metres (39 ft) above

high water level. A 40 foot tower
was built here in 1795 to warn ships
but, as the lantern at the top of the
tower was only 24 metres (79 ft)
above sea level, it could not be seen
in very big seas! Even when it was
replaced with a higher lighthouse
in the 1800s, ships continued to
founder there so anyone going past
this area needs to be exceptionally
careful. Fortunately for us, the sea
was relatively well behaved and the

Fishing Party

wind co-operating so that, by eleven o'clock, we were abeam of Longships
Light, passing this major landmark without incident. In keeping with tradition,
we prepared to pay homage to King Neptune as we went round Land's End.
Legend has it that one of his deputies is there and needs to be acknowledged.
Each member of the crew has to confess three sins – two privately and one
in public to the other crew members, then toss a coin over their left shoulder

Longships Lighthouse
© *A R Roberts, by kind permission*

48

into the sea. As tradition has it, "Not a brown coin, not a gold coin either, but something silver in between".

And so, with due homage paid, we passed Land's End but not before a large green roller came charging towards us. It was a big one, a one in twenty, about five or six metres tall and building. I felt a tremor of trepidation as I realized this was a breaking wave, and it was going to break right on top of us. We were not going to make it over the top but, in seconds, would find ourselves going through the wall of water and spume. Pat was down below so didn't really see it coming, but I was looking at it ... Claire was looking at it ...

We were all tethered securely to the boat and while I knew the boat would pop out the other side, I also knew it was going to be a very wet experience indeed. At the last minute, I yelled "Duck!" and dashed under the spray hood.

Claire, like a rabbit caught in the headlights, froze and took the full force of the greenie 'SMACK!' in the face! I looked up after it passed from where I had hastily taken shelter, huddled beneath the spray hood, to see her sprawled in the cockpit, pale, drenched, and literally gobsmacked. I always wondered where the meaning for that word came from and now I know!

I thought for a moment she was going to lose it but Pat looked at me, I looked at him, we both looked at Claire and suddenly we were all roaring with laughter!

We hadn't had time to put lee boards in the companionway to stop excess water rolling inside and, luckily, didn't really need to as the outboard well built into the floor of the cockpit allows for water to drain away incredibly fast, much better than other boats with only narrow drain holes.

Luckily, by this time, I had also pegged up the drain holes in the cockpit combing alongside the main hatch with pieces of cork so we didn't have streams of water in the main salon but the anchor well was still filling with water, draining into the boat and keeping the forepeak very wet.

We were round Longships at last and, while there is an inside passage, like the Manacles at Falmouth, it's for locals only really so we went around the outside. It was a lee shore and if the engine had cut out, or wind suddenly changed direction we could have found ourselves washed up on the rocks and, as history has shown us, rocks take no prisoners.

I have always had an opinion about rocks and hazards and that is that they're just there. If you go to sea, you'd better be ready and prepared. You're entering their environment. Don't blame them if you come to grief, if you find yourself at the wrong place at the wrong time. It's not their fault. Don't blame them.

Britain's coastline is full of corners and every corner has rocks. Rocks have no friends or enemies … they're just there. The rock doesn't mean any harm but, if you mess with it, … watch out, because they're hard, they're sharp and they'll bite your arse.

Britain is an old country, and with the sea pounding away at its edges for century after century there are great miles of coastline where, yes, the land starts at the waters edge, but the edge is in fact a twenty or thirty metre sheer cliff. One of the key problems I had was finding a place to put in each night as in some cases there was no gap in the cliff face, past which we were sailing. If there was, the coast was usually guarded by the slowly eroding, but nevertheless jagged teeth of rocky outcrops. Britain is not known for its sandy beaches and great care had to be taken to have several options for each day should the weather change.

By four o'clock, we were off St Ives, which has a large drying harbour and, at low tide, all the boats take the ground and sit on the mud, moored fore and aft. We had arrived at low tide so couldn't get in and had to anchor off the edge of the seawall, waiting for the tide to return.

Claire, who had, by then, recovered from her drenching, was sitting in the cockpit looking quietly pleased with herself about the fact that she had survived such a dramatic day. As we sat at anchor I said to her quietly, "Claire, don't move suddenly but quietly turn and have a look over your left shoulder."

She slowly turned, and found herself face to face with a large curious seal who had popped up out of the water to have a look at us. Well … that was it!

Claire melted in the cockpit and, through her tears, she said "Mike, you've brought me on the toughest thing I've ever done in my life. If

Welcome to St Ives

I'd known it was going to be a quarter as tough as it turned out to be, I would never have dreamt of coming with you, but you've looked after me, you've shown me some of the secrets of going to sea, and to be finally welcomed by a wild animal like that! It's been an absolutely magical day... Thank you so much!"

That evening, when the tide came back in, we put the boat up on the beach inside the tiny harbour and let her dry out. Claire had to get back to work so we climbed down off the boat onto the sand and walked her ashore, where she was met by her partner Simon. Then I had to negotiate, finally, the wretched repair to the anchor well drains, to stop the fo'c'sle, the forward part of the boat, from getting drenched.

We found a local marine engineer, Gary Aston from Marine Tech, who identified the problems with the bow of the boat. Not only did the fittings used at either end of the draining hose pipe not match properly but the diameter of the holes and pipe were too small to allow any water to drain away quickly. An anchor well full of water adds a lot of unnecessary weight at the front end of the boat, which seriously affects her handling capabilities, and I needed to get it fixed.

"Who made this crap?" Gary asked.

"Bob Brown"

"Nice boat," he said, "but these fittings are rubbish!"

That morning coming out of Penzance, I had had enough of the water up the front of the boat and had rung Bob to complain again. Bob simply

Sorting that wretched leak ... Gary Aston of Marine Tech

51

wouldn't accept that there was a problem.

"Bob, it's going to be fixed and you're paying for it," I said in frustration, "I'm taking your boat round some of the wildest coastline in Britain. I don't need it to fill up with water from the outside. We've got to keep the inside dry. I haven't got time to sail a tidal gate, fundraise in a pub and spend half

Celebrating the end of the leak …

the night cleaning up your shit. I've got to rest and I've got to be able to keep the stuff dry."

"Oh well," he said "Keep the receipt, send it to me and I'll think about it."

"Bob, you will pay it," I stated, and hung up the phone. I was very, very angry.

"This is just never going to work," said Gary upon closer inspection, so he ripped it all out and rebuilt it, working late into the night using proper fittings and hoses to keep it watertight. I was most disappointed with the attitude of Bob from Honnor Marine who was reluctant to admit there was a problem, let alone pay to have it repaired. The boat was still under warranty for heaven's sake, and it wasn't even watertight! The problem was however fixed and at last we would be able to use the forward area without everything getting drenched.

Hooray! And Bob did eventually refund me for the work …

Despite the issues with getting the leak fixed St Ives was a great place. We received a rapturous welcome from Martin Potter, who had organised a media call involving a story and photo shoot with the local newspaper, showers at his amazing house (a seven storey house built into the cliff overlooking the Bay), and many beers in the world famous and very ancient Sloop Inn where we sat by the harbour wall with a pint and I sang sea shanties as night fell:

Farewell and adieu to you fair Spanish Ladies,
Farewell and adieu to you ladies of Spain;
For we've received orders to sail for old England;
And we hope in a short time to see you again.
 Chorus:
 We'll rant and we'll roar like true British sailors,
 We'll range and we'll roar across the salt seas,
 Until we strike soundings in the Channel of old England,
 From Ushant to Scilly, 'tis thirty-five leagues.

Then we hove our ship to, with the wind in the sou'-west,
Then we hove our ship to, for to strike soundings clear;
We had forty–five fathoms and a fine sandy bottom,
So we filled the main topsail and up Channel did steer.
 Chorus
The first land we made was a point called the Dodman,
Next Rame Head near Plymouth, Start, Portland and Wight;
We sailed by Beachy, by Fairlee and Dungeness,
Where we bore right away for the South Foreland light.
 Chorus
Now the signal was made for the Grand Fleet to anchor,
All on the Downs the ships to be moored;
Let go your shank painter, stand by your cat stopper,
Haul up your clew garnets, stick out tacks and sheets.
 Chorus
Now let every man toss off his full bumper,
Let every man swig off a full bowl;
For we'll drink and be jolly and drown melancholy,
With 'Three cheers for the King and each true hearted soul.'
 Chorus

DAY 14 – 18TH JULY - ST IVES TO PADSTOW

Once afloat again, it was up anchor at 8 am and away out of St Ives, past Godrevy Island, another large rock with a unsavoury past and necessary lighthouse, so of course we were sailing well offshore, taking great care along the treacherous and exposed North Cornwall coast. We wanted to make sure we had plenty of room to manoeuvre for this coast, in particular, has a history full of shipwrecks and calamity and, should you be washed ashore, there are few open beaches but rather the jagged teeth of rocks below sheer cliffs, which are next to impossible to climb. A boat is by nature a sea creature and, while man enjoys the comforts found on land, boats and land do not mix well and should be avoided at all cost.

Past Newquay and over the Doom Bar, aptly named no doubt, then up the Camel River to Padstow.

Another day, another 35 miles or more.

Now most people would think – "Ha! 35, 40 miles, that's nothing. I can drive that in less than an hour in my car."

Well, try doing it at 3 miles per hour. These were big days, even when the weather and sea conditions were perfect, which was rare! Most people look at a map and measure the distance in a straight line. Like cars on roads that twist and turn as they negotiate the contours of the land, boats travel many miles in various directions in order to reach their destination, particularly when the wind is on the nose as it seemed to have been for almost my entire voyage so far.

In order to move straight ahead when you are sailing and the wind is coming towards you, a boat has to tack or beat to windward. Sailing to windward requires, above all, a lot of concentration as the helmsman must make constant minute adjustments in order to keep the boat sailing at its best. A good helmsman can "feel" the boat and respond to the amount of pressure he or she can feel through the tiller. In order to keep moving forward, the sails have to be kept at the right angle to the wind or the boat will stall, with sails flapping or, worse still, become overpowered and capsize! Sailing to windward involves a lot more work than sailing when the wind is coming from behind. The boat has to sail on an angle out to the right side of the course and then swing or tack back on an angle to sail up the left side of the course, crossing the centre line, or what is effectively the most direct route each time. Every time the boat switches tack or direction, the helmsman uses the tiller to push the rudder and turn the boat towards the new direction. As the boat changes course, the main sail moves across the boat, sometimes flogging as it catches the wind from the new direction, and the headsail, if used must be winched from one side of the boat, across the front of the mast to the other side. There are lots of things to do at once and the skipper and crew need to be on their toes.

As we sailed up the Camel River we were greeted by a small flotilla of boats from Padstow Sailing Club. Jon, David the Commodore and Barbara saw us safely to our mooring and welcomed us in with a massive farmhouse Cornish cream tea.

When we came ashore at the town quay, there was Stephanie, Pat's wife, ready to collect him after two weeks at sea with me. What a great companion he was!

At last, I had a day off. Time to dry out, fix some bits and pieces, get organised for the next leg of the journey and just sit, if only for a few minutes doing nothing, a luxury I had long gone without. I was exhausted, but elated. Two weeks of stressful adventure, but with fabulous companions who had kept my spirits high.

Hooray, hooray, hooray, at last the forepeak could dry out and what's more, stay dry!

CHAPTER 8 – OSCAR

Oscar Nowak joined me in Padstow. Oscar had learnt to sail with me on a delivery trip across the Atlantic to the Canaries and was an enthusiastic 28 year old, who could climb the rigging of a boat like a monkey, which came in handy later when we needed repairs up the mast.

He turned up and gave me a wave from the dock, so I rowed over to pick him up. "Yep," he said, "I've started the film." Turns out that the opening scene was of me rowing across to get him!

"Mike," he said when he got on board, "I've got a CD for you. It's Tiff Merrit." Tiff is a very beautiful country and western singer, and Oscar was obviously enamoured of her. I still have the CD today and often play it in the car.

The first thing we did, once he had dumped his stuff (which didn't take long), was go ashore for a feed at Rick Stein's Fish 'n Chip shop. Rick is a local celebrity chef who probably employs 50 or 60 people in his shop, café and restaurant, doing wonders for the local community. Where else can you get oysters and white wine for £6.50?

DAY 15 – 19TH JULY - PADSTOW

The next morning members of the Padstow Sailing Club took us for a

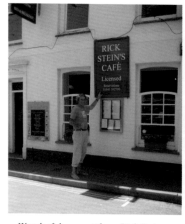

Wonderful support from Rick Stein

Rick Stein's gourmet Fish 'n Chips Padstow

trip in the club boat up the Camel River to Wadebridge, where we had fish 'n chips for lunch.

They had kindly offered to do an evening fund raiser for us so once again I was in need of raffle prizes. I wandered up to Tesco and chatted up the manager, who kindly donated some wine. He also had a whole lot of end-of-season beach kit, a shelter, inflatable ten pin bowling, and other bits and pieces and I came away laden down. Thank you Mr Tesco!

I organised a round of golf at the local club, Fight for Sight T-shirts, mugs and pens. I always tried to get 10 prizes so people felt they had a chance of winning something.

High and Dry on Padstow Sands.

I went to see Mr Stein himself, but he wasn't there so I talked to his manageress. She said she was sure he would like to help so gave me a card entitling the bearer to "Coffee and Cakes for Two" at Rick Stein's Café – a mystery prize.

Everyone wanted to know what was in the mystery prize.

"You'll just have to buy more tickets and find out," I told them.

The club was fantastic. We had burgers and a barbecue, and it was a lovely experience with lots of people wanting to help. We got to the draw for the star prize and the lady who had done all the cooking ended up winning the mystery prize. Everyone thought that it was great.

Grand Draw at Padstow Sailing Club.

Oscar and I decided that in order to catch the tide in the morning we would sail to the mouth of the river, past the bar and anchor overnight under the headland. This meant we could get away early without having to deal with the Doom Bar. It did however mean we had to mount an anchor watch, one hour and a half on and the same asleep. I insisted on an anchor watch any night we were not on a mooring or tied up safely. This was split between the number of crew on board. On this occasion unfortunately that meant two.

People often asked me how we got on for food on board the boat, enquiring whether I could get a cup of tea made or cook up some grub. The trick was to keep it simple. The boat was set up with a sort of amidships catering station. There was no gimballed stove, but I did have a base tray which held a camping stove on the right side of the cabin. On the left was a rudimentary sink, but it had no drain. The drain consisted of picking it up and taking it outside to tip it overboard – it was a dog bowl really, so not really large enough for much more than a small dunk and slosh. Up forward was a 10 litre water tank which connected to a pump tap. This turned out to be more effort than it was worth so water was just poured from bottles when needed.

There was a little box fridge, which couldn't be used at sea as it would drain the batteries, but was connected occasionally when we had dockside power to keep things fresh.

Bear in mind that we made port of some kind each evening so really only relied on the catering facilities for breakfast, cups of tea and lunch, and the occasional emergency supper.

Saving our crustacean – The Lobster Hatchery in Padstow

Food was simple too. We would start the day with a good cup of tea, served in bed to all crew members by the skipper. This was usually followed up with a hearty serving of Brookie's porridge, or toast made over the gas burner, accompanied by a glass of orange juice and a banana, or other appropriate fruit. I say appropriate because I have learnt over the years at sea that some foods seem to have an undesired affect on the digestive system and are more likely to make you seasick, so are best avoided.

In the old days, sailors used to deal with sea sickness by eating hard tack, which were dense biscuits, often containing unwanted guests such as weevils. When the rocking motion of a boat upsets the equilibrium in the ear, a side effect is an increase in stomach acid. Eating a biscuit, particularly a ginger one, neutralises the stomach acid and helps to keep the stomach settled.

I have always discouraged people from drinking coffee, which again increases the acidity of your stomach and, if you're feeling slightly queasy, makes you spew. Apples are not good for the same reason. I always make sure there is a good supply of snacks, sweetie bars, jaffa cakes, and bikkies, especially ginger bikkies. The trick is to look after yourself and make sure you don't become a casualty. Seasickness can put you in serious danger, not only physically, if the nausea is not stopped and essential minerals and fluids are not replaced, but also by seriously limiting your ability to operate and function in a safe and effective way.

Smells, tiredness, claustrophobia, all sorts of things can get you started. The best thing you can do if feeling slightly queasy is to sit outside in the fresh air where you can focus on the horizon. Hot Tip ... just like the astronauts at Cape Canaveral, take a Stugeron (available at any chemist) the night before you sail and top up at breakfast and, thereafter, every 4 hours or so until you find your sea legs. And avoid the hooch too ...

Leaving Padstow – fabulous welcome, support and send off by the members of Padstow Sailing Club

DAY 16 – 20ᵀᴴ JULY - PADSTOW TO BUDE

At half past five the next morning we were up with the dawn, bound for Bideford, a good day's sail of nearly 50 miles. It seemed a lot but we had to set a target or we were never going to get anywhere. By eight o'clock, we were motor sailing on a very uneven sea, making much slower progress than we had hoped for. We knew the boat had been through worse but, when you're pounding up and down, hour after hour, lack of mile after lack of mile, you can only sustain the effort for so long. We were wet, we were salt encrusted, we were tired and the endless coastline seemed to be completely stationary. Frustration grew as the tide turned against us and we knew there was no way we would make it to Bideford by the end of the day. We had to consider our options.

We decided to go in and have a look at a little place called Bude. The coast there is very exposed and from the sea all you could see was what appeared to be big rolling waves breaking up on the beach, but we knew there was a small canal that comes down through a lock with a tiny little set of moorings. It was just a matter of finding the entrance from the sea. Note to mariners: this is not to be contemplated in strong onshore winds.

The wind was from the west – yes onshore, the sea was lumpy, the current was against us, and morale was low.

Oh shit! What could we do?

It may have been safest to stay at sea and sit it out, hove-to offshore, but I looked at Oscar, he looked at me and we thought we'd give it a go. Neither of us fancied sailing any further, especially out into deep water and then facing a restless night taking turns on watch while we floated about waiting for daylight. We identified the entrance to the channel and it looked negotiable. I thought I'd be able to spin the boat round and get out if needed, after all, fishermen don't put moorings in places that

Watch those breakers and keep a safe distance

60

Safely tied up at Bude

are too dangerous so I figured there must be a reason to give it a go. We got ourselves prepared.

We dropped the sails but had them ready to go in case we had any problems with the engine. We had the main anchor ready to drop, and got the second kedge anchor ready in case it all turned to custard. At least that way we might be able to stop ourselves smashing into a solid object. We went in carefully and positively, came round the corner on a wave, unsure about what we would find, and suddenly there was the row of moorings.

When I saw how much the tide surged in and out I realised I was probably unable to get the anchor to hold in the outgoing current of the river. To top it off we were both exhausted and I wanted a good night's kip.

I saw a possible mooring and said to Oscar,

"We've got one chance at this. You have to pick up the mooring first go. This is no time to be cack-handed. Don't go for the handle, go for the rope. I don't care what's growing on it. I don't care how much slime it has. Grab the rope and take a turn round the Samson post. Do you read my lips Oscar?"

"Yes, boss, yes," came back the reply.

"Then bugger off down the front, if you please, and get ready."

I keep my boat hook in a tube alongside the boom so it's always ready to use; he stood at the front, armed with the boathook, ready to swing.

Tortured Wood and Stone at Bude

There was no room to come up neatly and swing around, it was more a case of coming up, hammering into reverse just in front of the buoy and hoping like hell that Oscar could hook the rope.

First go … he missed!

I let the surf wash us forward.

"Oscar, get your arse out on the front of the boat and I'll get you even closer."

Second sweep, and he grabbed it.

The rope was round the Samson post quick as greased lightning. The relief of being attached to something and not washed up on the beach or bashed against the harbour wall was huge. We tied the boat up properly, cut the engine, swung round, and suddenly everything was quiet. We looked at each other and collapsed laughing.

Across on the beach a man with his dog watched us.

"I just saw that," he called, "That was a good effort, but you shouldn't be there at all!"

"I know," I said, "I don't need to be told and I totally agree with you!"

"Tell you what," he said, "I own the Grosvenor B & B up the top there. Get yourselves squared away and come up and see us in an hour's time for a bath and a fry up."

That was not what I had expected – I thought he was going to offer us up to the local authorities but, instead, he offered us a feed. The kindness of strangers!

We got everything stowed, pumped up the dinghy and rowed ashore. At the top of the hill we knocked on the door and met Will and Helen Shingler.

"Go and have a bath," they said.

Well, what can I say? How fabulous!

And yes, for the second time on the trip … I fell asleep in the bath.

I was woken once again by a thumping on the door and Oscar calling, "Come on Mike, the bacon will be burnt to a crisp if you don't hurry up!"

We ate ourselves silly on afternoon bacon and eggs.

"Where did you say you come from … Bosham?" Will asked.

"Yes that's right," I said.

"Oh, what a coincidence," he said, "my brother lives there." What a small world! To this day, his brother, Robert, runs past our house with his dog, most mornings, and always gives us a wave.

We went back to the boat feeling much better.

We didn't fund-raise in Bude, we survived.

Storm clouds brewing (again!) North Cornwall

DAY 17 – 21ST JULY – BUDE TO LUNDY ISLAND

The next morning I got up and found that the dinghy had disappeared off the front of the boat. "Oh no, where the hell could it have gone?" I said, feeling very perplexed.

"Don't worry," said Oscar, "Look!"

There was a huge sea lock that was open at the seaward end but the lock gates were shut at the canal end, with a chain across them as this wasn't a working lock. I'd asked Will about it and he said it took three months' notice to get the canal end gates open so it only happened very rarely, when a large boat needed to go inland.

Oscar Nowak at Bude

There, bouncing up against the canal gates, was our dinghy and I had to roll my trouser legs up to my bum and wade through the slimy grubby water to get the boat. Not what I wanted to do after my lovely bath the day before!

CHAPTER 9 – HEADING NORTH …

The bad weather had passed. The wind for once wasn't on the nose. Hallelujah!

It was still predominantly from the west, but we had a reasonably pleasant sail on a reach across to the Island of Lundy, a lump of granite about 400 feet high, lying off the coast where the Bristol Channel meets the Atlantic Ocean.

The Island itself is long and narrow, 3½ miles long by half a mile wide, and runs north to south so the west side is exposed to the might of the Atlantic and the east side is relatively sheltered.

We made good progress, for a change, and had nearly reached our destination, coming round Surf Point, aptly named, when …

Bang! Crash!

The gaff fell down and landed between us. We looked at each other in shock. The gaff is not a light piece of wood and it dawned on us both that either of us could have been killed or at least seriously injured, had it fallen to one side or the other.

I looked up at the top of the mast and saw that the bolt going through the top of the mast holding the peak and genoa halyards had lost its nut and some of the fittings had fallen away. We had to find somewhere to make some temporary repairs and headed for the nearest sheltered spot. There were some nasty currents around the rocks guarding the bay we had chosen

Fine yachting with the Caymans Gennaker

Moored in Lundy Bay

but it was reasonably calm so we motored in past a platoon of seals basking on the rocks beneath the lighthouse, picked our way carefully over to a calm spot in the lee of the surrounding cliffs and hooked a mooring buoy. The first thing I did when we got in, having apologised profusely to Oscar, regained my composure and, metaphorically speaking, changed my pants, was to send Oscar up the mast to have a look and see if he could fix it.

This wasn't easy as the masthead was still equipped with two of the original blocks, not the new Barton ones.

Masthead repairs at Lundy, Oscar aloft …

I knew they wouldn't cope well with too much strain, which is why I had changed all the other blocks around the boat. These were the last two original blocks and I hadn't had the time, or the assistance necessary, to climb the mast and change them before I left.

For once, the water was calm as the wind, which continued to blow outside the bay, was blocked by the rugged landform towering above us. This was fortunate as climbing a mast is daunting at the best of times but, when it has to be done in the open sea, with the wind blowing and boat tossing up and down, the job becomes an awful lot harder as the craft sways from side to side, seemingly trying to fling the hapless climber into the water.

All repaired – not pretty but hopefully strong enough

I sent Oscar up the mast using the Genoa halyard at the front that was still attached to the nut-less bolt at the top. Oscar is very strong and agile and he said, "Don't

View from the top

worry Mike, I'll climb the mast myself and only use the bosun's chair and the halyard as a keeper. It'll take my weight if I need it."

So he shimmied up the mast, semi climbing it. I had some spare nuts and other bits and pieces down below and Oscar was able to attach a replacement nut onto the bolt, which surprisingly, still seemed to be straight and true.

Mr Sod had left us alone for a while so I suppose it was to be expected that he would raise his ugly head again and, sure enough, as Oscar was at the top of the mast, the rope slipped down the side of the block and jammed. Fortunately Oscar could climb like a monkey and was able to get up and down without

Safely back on deck

having to rely on the faulty block. Needless to say we replaced both of the old ones and, while I needed to get it checked later to see that there were no other complications, I was satisfied that it would last us for the remainder of the voyage and, indeed, I haven't had the same problem again.

By teatime, we were sorted again so we sat and caught our breath, had a can of beer each and then went ashore to explore the island and see if we could find some puffins, appropriate perhaps with the name of the island supposedly coming from

the Norse word for Puffin. The island is a rat free nature reserve, known for its fantastic bird and marine life. Unfortunately for Oscar, try as we might, we didn't get to see one puffin the entire time we were on or near the island. The Lundy Island puffins had decamped for another spot.

DAY 18 – 22ND JULY – LUNDY ISLAND

The next day, we went ashore again and walked over large

Puffins, Lundy Island
© *David Chapman, www.davidchapman.org.uk*
Reprinted by kind permission

parts of the Island. We visited the Trinity House lighthouse, saw some deer and the remains of a crashed Luftwaffe plane from the Second World War but no puffins.

The Island has a rollicking history; it was used by the Knights Templar, British and later Barbary pirates, it was a prison and even had its own king at one time with its own currency, aptly named the puffin and the half puffin. It was eventually sold in 1969 to Jack Hayward, a British millionaire, who paid £150,000 for it and donated it to the National Trust, which then leased it to the Landmark Trust, which has converted many of the old vacant structures, such as the castle and former lighthouse, into basic accommodation, which you can book.

As we climbed a track on our way back, I saw a flag flying from the castle. Assuming it was part of the National Trust, I knocked at the door of one of the buildings to see if we could get a ticket to look around the castle. "Oh no," we were told, "This is the Landmark Trust and we've rented the castle and are staying here with our families."

Lundy fund raising

We were quickly introduced to two doctors with their wives and what seemed like a moving mass of children – but then I suppose doctors know all about biology so are pretty good at creating the next generation! They invited us in for a yummy snack of scones with jam and clotted cream.

I said to the kids, "Who would like a present?"

"We'd like a present!"

"Right, well you'll have to come down to the boat and you will have to answer a question about lifeboats."

"Can we go? Can we go?"

In the end they all came and we had a party onboard. I brought *Theo's Future* closer to the beach and got the anchor to hold. We ended up with 21 people onboard!

68

Oscar and I, two doctors and their wives and fifteen children! Turns out the children didn't all belong to the doctors, as some of them had brought a friend with them. Our little boat wasn't designed to hold so many people. The water was six inches deep in the cockpit, and no one could move around too much! Time for sedentary activities and I told them about our adventures so far and why we were trying to raise money. The kids wrote some stories and drew some lovely pictures, one even showed a submarine!

Each of the kids got a dip in the lucky dip bag and the parents gave us a great donation.

Later that evening, two of the kids came down to the beach and shouted across the water, "Mike, Mike, are you there?"

"Hello," I called.

"We've got some of our supper to share with you, come and get it."

So we rowed ashore again and, sure enough, there was a lovely chicken curry in a tupperware container for us. Fabulous!

DAY 19 – 23ʀᴅ JULY – LUNDY ISLAND TO TENBY

Next morning we motored clear of the rocks and set sail to South Wales - where Tenby was substituted for Swansea 'cos that's the way the wind was blowing.

What a day! We had a spanking reach all the way across the Bristol Channel, heading north across what is known to be a treacherous piece of water, with huge currents and wild waves. King Neptune must have decided we needed a bit of a break, as we blasted across, making nearly fifty miles, a full day's

sailing, right into the delightful harbour of Tenby in the south of Wales. The town, made up mainly of 18th century town houses and famous for its seafood, is built into the cliffs overlooking the harbour. We tied up beside a little boat in the harbour, where the tide went out and left us sitting on the mud.

Oscar had spent the whole day on the helm and complained of having a sore arm. Aaahhh, clearly

Sleigh ride along South Wales coast

Sister Mary!

a candidate for some Commando training to toughen him up!

In Tenby we were joined by my little sister Mary, who, like us, arrived in town quite late, so much so that the pubs were shut and we just managed to grab a Doner Kebab before the whole place closed for the night.

DAY 20 - 24TH JULY – TENBY TO DALE

We were up very early the next morning, not only because we were hungry, but because poor Mary was in desperate need of a pee. Wanting to maintain a level of dignity and decorum in a boat full of men, she was reluctant to use the bucket and so was incredibly keen to get ashore.

The boat was sitting on the mud so we used the boarding ladder to climb down to the mud and walked to the harbour wall, dragging the dinghy with us so we could get back later when the tide had turned.

My little sister is Head of the English Department at a very large grammar school so is used to having her say.

We climbed the sea wall to the public toilets and found the cleaner at work who said, "Sorry they're closed, Come back later."

This was not what she wanted to hear.

"No, YOU don't understand. I HAVE TO GO!" said Mary

It would take a very brave man indeed to stand his ground when Mary was in an adamant mood.

"Oh! All right then, you'd better go in," said the cleaner, scurrying out of her way.

Well, she went in looking very tense and came out looking very relieved, with dignity restored.

Right, problem number one sorted. Now for food.

Nice cuppa with Oscar Nowak and my sister Mary

Bear in mind it was only six in the morning and, when we walked through town, there wasn't anything open. We had time to kill so what better way to pass the time than to check out the acoustics of the marvellous bandstand and, yes, sing sea shanties! Even Mary, who normally pours scorn on her big brother's efforts joined in with the chorus.

As we later walked back down towards the harbour, my nose was enthralled by the smell of bacon cooking. The olfactory nerve is a powerful thing; it is however one thing to smell something and quite another to find out where it is coming from. I'd gone ahead to sniff out the bacon and found a small hole-in-the-wall kiosk, where I ordered three double bacon baps with mustard and three teas and coffees. I went back to find Oscar and Mary and told them I'd had no luck but they didn't believe me!

As we were sitting munching our baps down by the harbour, we overheard a couple of old fisherman sharing a funny story at the other end of the bench we were sitting on, about one of their mates who had got cross at a seagull that had dropped its load on his shoulder. While trying to clean it up, he overbalanced in his dinghy and fell overboard, headfirst! They thought this was hilarious and the story was told so well, with such lovely local accents, that so did we. Tenby was lovely and it really would have been nice to stay, and in fact we almost did …

We only just managed to leave Tenby Harbour, as I had misjudged the tide. I had to get Mary and Oscar to move forward while I quickly jumped overboard to give the boat a push off the mud, and we slithered off as the last of the water drained out towards the harbour entrance. Phew!

We were sailing out past the sea wall when Mary felt a thud of something heavy hit her in the shoulder and fall to the deck. One of the local fishermen hadn't looked to see if it was clear, when he cast his

Bacon butties going down a treat

71

line, and Mary had been hit by the lead weight at the end of his fishing line. She was very lucky it hadn't hit her in the head, and she was, quite rightly, furious! We still have the end of the line, complete with weight, which we cut from the fisherman's trace. One has to wonder whether this was an accident. There is no love lost between fishermen and sailors. I was sure I had left plenty of room between the sea wall and us but you never know.

We sailed south, past Caldey Island, famous for its monastery and, of course, another lighthouse, and turned towards the west, making for the Milford Haven estuary and the River Cleddau. Milford Haven was once one of the biggest ports in Britain because of its position on the river. The watercourse bends sufficiently to protect the area from sea swells and strong coastal winds, and it is also deep and wide, able to accommodate huge supertankers and, as a result, became an important centre for the oil industry.

Out at sea, I was looking forward to the shelter of the river because it had been a long day. The wind, fortunately, was from the east so we had a good reaching sail, past St Govan's Head and on past Linney Island. The waves, however, were looming large and big waves, even when only rolling along with plenty of space in between, are still quite intimidating when you are in a small boat. You sit in the cockpit, tiller clenched firmly, dealing with the uneven puffs of wind that erratically come and go as the waves rise up and

Dried out in Tenby

72

interrupt the flow of the breeze. The waves, meanwhile, rise before you and you need to concentrate on riding the back of the wave at a good angle so that the boat cuts cleanly through the top of the wave before descending into the trough ahead. It sometimes doesn't pay to look behind as the wave you have just shot down the front of rises up behind you and almost seems to be attempting to catch you up. When one particularly persistent wave nearly came into the cockpit from behind, I really had had enough and was quite relieved when we sailed into the estuary and round the corner to a quiet spot called Dale, supposedly the sunniest place in Britain. We arrived too late for pub grub but the sailing club welcomed us with open arms and, after three portions of shepherd's pie, washed down with a fair amount of red wine, we were anybody's!

DAY 21 – 25ᵀᴴ JULY – DALE TO NEYLAND

We got up the next morning to be met by a soggy world and sheets of rain, which fortunately cleared fairly quickly, and the day improved further after a delightful experience with the local sailing school children.

I asked the instructor if we could explain to the children what we were doing and they all gathered round to listen to our story.

One of the kids asked, "What's it like to be blind?"

"I'll tell you what," I said, "Try and rig one of these boats with your eyes closed."

So they did and it was a shambles.

Before we had any injuries or accidents, we got them to stop and open their eyes. They had a pretty good, quick appreciation for what it meant to be blind.

Next came a tear jerking moment.

One of the little boys said "My mum gave me 50p to get a Mars Bar at break time. I want to give it to you for Theo."

Then another child offered his pocket money too, then another and another. Soon I had nearly ten quid, all given to me by the small children who wanted to help us with our efforts. Wonderful!

They invited us to join them on their sailing expedition down the river for a barbecue but we had to keep going as Mary needed to catch a train and get back to work. We said our farewells and off we went up the river past Milford Haven to Neyland, where Mary departed. She left me a note saying, "I'm more than sure that the required sum for the scanner will be reached, given

Mike's ability to make friends with anyone who looks at the boat. A great two days, very many thanks, Love Mousey."

I had an organised media engagement at Neyland the next day so we cleaned and tidied up the boat. Things had got very disorganised and dishevelled, not to mention a bit pongy, and I wanted the boat to be gleaming bright and smelling sweet when the press arrived, which they did in due course, and I was interviewed by Pembroke Radio. We also had to wait for Daisy Wylam, our next sailing companion, to join us. We took the opportunity while stopped at Neyland to repair the hull damage inflicted when the anchor and chain got loose sailing out past the Needles. What a long time ago that seemed to be!

A Good Luck Card

DAY 22 – 26TH JULY – NEYLAND

Our hosts at Neyland, Jeff and Sarah Browning, couldn't have been kinder. Sarah processed a massive bundle of filthy clothes through her washing machine for us and she and Jeff, who had 20 years Charter Skipper experience in the Caribbean, even collected Daisy Wylam from the station. By the time Daisy arrived, she was very fortunate to be greeted by a spic and span vessel and crew.

Buffing out the storm damage ...

Another healthy contribution ...

CHAPTER 10 – A LOT OF HARD WORK

DAY 23 – 27ᵀᴴ JULY – NEYLAND TO SALVA TO WHITESAND

We left the next morning while it was still dark with a couple of hours sailing ahead of us to get back down the river. The sun was coming up as we made our way out of the estuary to St Anne's Head and back to the open sea. We had been warned by a local lifeboatman, Frank Penfold, that, while we could safely sail inside Skokholm and then through Jack Sound, if we were really careful, we should only attempt it with the tide, in calm weather. Jack Sound is about a third of a mile wide and separates the mainland from Skomer Island and a number of smaller islands and rocks that seem to always be found around such areas. The tidal race through here is known to be ferocious at times and it is not unusual to see up to 8 knots of tide rushing through, even when the weather is relatively fine. Luckily that day it was overcast but calm.

The aim was to get through Jack Sound, across St Bride's Bay, through Ramsey Sound and round to Fishguard. I was keen to get this part of the coast behind me as it had a fearsome reputation, with several famous tales of ship wrecks and calamity originating from the area. For some reason I felt a sense of unease and, while my brain was telling me "Nonsense!" there was a part of me that wasn't keen to see what lay ahead.

Frank had been kind enough to draw a chart for me and so we had no problems finding our way around the corner and through Jack Sound. I could see, though, why he had mentioned caution as there were several rocks we may not have seen, had we not known to look out for them.

With Jack Sound safely behind us we sped across St Bride's Bay where we were joined by a pod of dolphins that delighted us with their antics as they followed us

Master Mariner Frank's essential advice ...

along. No sooner had they lost interest in us and swum away than we suddenly found ourselves surrounded by a huge flotilla of birds floating about on the water. Oscar cut a mean course through them to discover they were puffins. How amazing! Probably the missing puffins from Lundy Island.

But, as we approached Ramsey Sound, I realised we were in trouble ...

We'd timed it that we had to be low water plus two to get across the bay to Ramsey Sound, which is guarded on the northern side by a particularly nasty set of rocks aptly known as 'The Bitches'. Described as a set of teeth that spanned half the channel in the Sound, ready to chew up anyone foolish enough to get sucked towards them, I had never seen them for myself, but was not at all keen to get a close look!

It had taken us longer than expected to cross St Bride's Bay and, as we approached Ramsey Sound, I sensed that the tide had turned against us. Should we take a punt and have a go at getting through the Sound relying on the little 5 hp outboard engine?

I knew that, even if we got through to the north, we could still be swept back onto 'The Bitches' should the engine fail, and they had their reputation for a reason. I wasn't prepared to take the risk and, with much disappointment, we turned away just short of Ramsey Sound and made our way into the little port and town of Solva. We threw the hook down and I suddenly felt so dejected. I was tired after a long and stressful morning and my morale was very low. I do not like to fail in achieving my goals and I was very aware that each day I fell behind schedule had to be made up at some stage, if the entire trip were to stay on target. I had crew booked to meet me at all parts of the country and, if I missed a day, it would mean sailing on one of my precious port days, which were much needed for restocking of fuel, supplies, energy and sanity.

Daisy and Oscar cheered me up. They pointed out that we had tried to bite off a big chunk, had got quite a long way and, with a good start

Daisy Wylam, a skilful helmsman

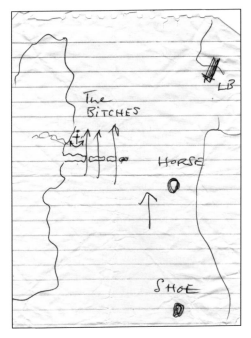

Ramsey Sound and the Bitches

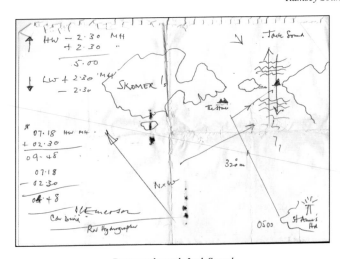

Passage through Jack Sound

when we were all feeling refreshed, we should still be able to make some more miles that day, once the tide had turned in our favour again.

"Have a little kip and we'll go ashore and get fuel and supplies," they suggested.

What a marvellous idea.

They rowed to shore and arrived back a couple of hours later, laden with food for lunch and supper, fuel, water and a story to tell. They had bumped into an extremely nice harbour master by the name of Anthony, who promptly offered them a lift to the garage and a brief glimpse of St David's Cathedral, which is a truly amazing, vast structure surrounded by a tiny village further up the coast. I would have liked to have gone with them but was probably better off having stayed behind for a nap. They assured me they'd said a prayer for me.

"Well as long as you got on your knees in there and had a little thought, that's fine," I said, grinning.

We motored out of Solva later that afternoon as, with daylight saving we still had several hours of light to see us on our way. We fortunately had the tide with us as we turned around the coast, helping to push us towards Ramsey Sound.

I had had a very unsettled feeling most of the day, the tides seemed to be doing strange things and, while there was some wind, it was erratic and inconsistent. I am not normally one for superstitions, but that day I felt a whisper of unease breathing down my neck and, by the time we got to Ramsey Sound and nearer 'The Bitches', well, I tell you, I didn't even like looking at them.

I'm usually pretty neutral about rocks, but these ones, well, they were real sons of bitches, aptly named if you ask me. There's something particularly nasty and scary about them and I bet they've claimed a few lives over the ages ... not a nice way to go.

What makes these rocks so wicked, you may ask ...

The water is funnelled between Ramsey Island and the mainland, and the Bitches form a reef, rather like a row of sharp incisor crocodile teeth that stretch out from the island, almost reaching the middle of the channel. With the rocks spread out in such a fashion, they form a kind of dam and the water on one side of the rocks is sometimes as much as one and a half metres higher than the water on the other side. With the water under this significant pressure, the speed at which it flows through the gaps is incredibly fast and has been known to reach 18 knots! To put this in perspective my 5 hp engine at full throttle can only do about 5 knots.

On a good day this area is popular with white water kayakers, so you can perhaps now understand why I wanted to keep well away from them and was extremely glad to get past, even though crossing the bay on the other side was very unpleasant indeed.

The wind was from the northwest, not quite on the nose, but enough to make our passage slow and lumpy. We weren't making a lot of progress, the day was fast drawing to a close and, once again, I didn't see how we could get round the headland and up the coast to Fishguard. I wasn't even sure that we wanted to, as the wind was rising and the tide was about to turn. Rather than face the open sea, or be washed backward across the bay, into the reach of 'The Bitches' once more, I decided to tuck us in at Whitesands Bay, which is a long sweeping sandy beach with a small cove at each end, providing some options for shelter should the wind change direction. We motored in and dropped the anchor.

By now the wind was beginning to howl and, if I was superstitious, I could almost think it was emanating from the rocks just to our south, howling their protest that we had escaped from their clutches. This was one place I didn't want the anchor to slip or drag, so we rowed out with the backup kedge anchor and another five metres of chain, which we set at an angle to make a crows foot. The halyards were slapping, the wind was whistling through the rigging and the waves could be heard crashing on the nearby rocks. Not the sort of sounds to lull you into a pleasant night of sleep, and to top it off, we all had a disjointed night with split anchor watches – one hour on, two off.

Despite signing up for the graveyard shift (2359 – 0130), I was allowed to sleep through! When quizzed, Oscar and Daisy just said that they thought I needed a few extra hours of kip – perhaps a gesture of self preservation.

DAY 24 – 28ᵀᴴ JULY – WHITESAND TO FISHGUARD

We were all awake early, the conditions were not such that you could relax; the gulls were crying, calling out to each other as they circled overhead, and the many noises of nature echoed around the bay. It was a cold and evil morning as dawn broke. We were all tired from the emotional strain of the day before and a sleepless night. The wind was still howling, seeming to swirl down off the cliffs and round our little boat as she tracked mile after mile, around and around her tether, which fortunately had held fast overnight.

So … I made us porridge!

Nothing like a bowl of Brookie's porridge to raise the spirits, gird the loins and rouse the crew.

Feeling more invigorated, we motored out past Strumble Head and up the exposed coast to Fishguard. The wind was still blasting from the northwest, hampering our progress so that time slowed and the day dragged out by the minute, broken only by the sheets of spray that doused us at irregular intervals, stinging our eyes as we rose and fell with the uneven timbre of the waves.

It was a wet and weary day and we were all glad to get to our destination and drop anchor for a well deserved rest.

Fishguard is a main ferry hub, with large ships ploughing across St George's Channel to Ireland and other faraway places, so rather than go where the big ships operated from, we motored across to the old harbour, where we were less likely to be disturbed by the noise and wake of the larger vessels.

There was a lovely Falmouth Pilot Cutter along the wharf with a large crowd of children aboard, so, seeing an opportunity for some fundraising, we blew up some of our 'Fight for Sight' balloons and gave them to the kids. The woman on board seemed very harassed and suspicious of our behaviour so we left it at that and went ashore

We bought provisions, and returned to the boat after a good pub supper and a refreshing pint or two, set for our onward journey the next day.

DAY 25 – 29TH JULY - FISHGUARD TO ABERAERON

Next day saw us back at sea, feeling much better in body, spirit and mind and we had a very pleasant day's sailing (for a change) up the coast to Aberaeron on the Welsh coast. A huge relief after the drama of the days before, and a reminder that, perhaps, it may not all be hard work after all.

Our initial attempt at fore and aft mooring in the fast receding tidal harbour was not that successful as there was poor holding for our Kedge anchor but Bill, the harbour master, came to our aid and tucked us into a neat spot that he had created for visitors, leaving us time to case the joint. What a delightful little place this turned out to be, with lots of lovely coloured houses built overlooking the harbour. Whilst there, we even managed a swim in the village pool, where Oscar kicked my butt after challenging me to a gentle two length 'any stroke will do' sprint. It was there, that I was bowled over by Daisy.

"Mike," she said, "This trip is like a dream come true and I know I'm studying for my competent crew ticket and that you won't sign me off 'till I've passed my exam at the end of the week. Well, this really isn't a form of bribery, but … I'd like to give the boat a present".

I said "Daisy, you're a student, you have no money for presents."

"Oh," she said, "I have a few pennies saved up," and she produced … a cuddly dolphin.

"There's just one condition Mike. I need to use the dolphin as a pillow 'cos it's damned uncomfortable up the front. So, as long as I can use it while I'm on the boat, you can keep it."

"Daisy," I said, "Perfect!"

As I voyaged around the country I tried to let the rest of the world know where I was, what I had been up to and how the journey was progressing through a regular blog which I emailed to Nick Sherman so he could update our webpage. This was not always easy to do as I had no internet access on the boat and had to rely on finding an internet café, or asking people I met if I could use their computer.

In Aberaeron, the task was made all the more complicated by the fact that the computer I had been offered to use, by a lovely couple we met at the quayside, had three keys that didn't work and I had to think of words that avoided using the affected letters so that the story made sense. I am not one for crosswords at the best of times so trying to think of similes when you're tired is quite hard work. I managed after much complicated word mongering to get the blog completed.

DAY 26 – 30ᵀᴴ JULY - ABERAERON TO PWLLHELI (PETHELLY)

The next day we set off across Cardigan Bay towards Pwllheli (pronounced Pethelly). I'd chosen to spend a night there for several reasons. I'd been there before, it's a pretty good harbour and I knew I wanted to stop somewhere at the top of Cardigan Bay before I attempted Bardsey Sound, which is another potential horror show. I wanted to be close enough that we could tackle it in the morning when we were fresh and had daylight, tide and time on our side.

The conditions that day were boisterous, with the wind from the west and big waves washing across the bay. The visibility was very poor and we all strained to see the Bell Buoy that marks the outer end of a huge sand bar towards the North of the bay. "There it is!" called out Daisy, pointing over to starboard through the murk – "That's great" I replied with some relief … finding the channel markers was essential, if we were to make our way safely round the hazard, so all of us were keyed up, eyes peeled. In this sort of situation you find yourself experiencing a kind of expectation tinged with fear. The adrenalin pumps through your system, and the excitement level rises as you take on the elements, placing faith in your skill and ability to overcome the associated risk. When suddenly you see your destination, in this case the entrance to Pwllheli harbour, the relief is amazing.

The swing of emotions on this trip was truly incredible and, while most times I had companions to share the workload, my role as skipper and captain perhaps added an extra burden with the need to ensure the sanity and safety of my crew. At times the crew were unaware of the danger we were in and, while this made their sailing experience enjoyable, the strain of maintaining a calm and positive persona on the outside was difficult at times when on the inside my mind was going *"Oh shit!"*

We had reached Pwllheli in darkness and rain, and parked the boat on a very convenient pontoon, pleased to have made safe haven at last. After a long day at sea we all went ashore for a much needed shower and reviving meal.

DAY 27 – 31ST JULY - PWLLHELI TO PORTH DINLLAEN

In the morning we set off on a very overcast, very gusty day. The weather was debatable but the wind and tide were right so I decided to proceed. We were on our way to tackle more strategic headlands, serious stuff, with rip tides and eddies to contend with.

We had gone some miles down the coast and were just past Abersoch when, suddenly, out of nowhere, the wind swung round 30 degrees and a 40 knot squall knocked us off course. What was going to be a safe passage around the nearby rocks turned into a lee shore, upon which I was being blown. We were literally stopped in our tracks and then being blown towards some very, very nasty rocks only 50 metres away. We were too close, too 'effing' close and getting closer by the second!

I dumped the mainsail, and started the engine all in one go. I don't think the others had a clue about how much danger we were in. I really had too much on my plate to notice what they thought as I charged around the boat systematically altering the sails and adjusting the engine and steering to make headway from near disaster. With the engine full on and a little stay sail, I managed to get the boat to change direction, on a reach back the way I'd come, and we clawed our way inch by inch away from the rocks. All this happened within minutes and it was only after we had a safe distance to catch our breath that I had time to reflect on how close we had got to catastrophe. I had the sudden realization that my little journey was actually a huge undertaking that would bite me on the arse, if I wasn't extremely careful. While I felt I had handled the situation as best I could, I was also aware that the days were mounting and, with them, a growing sleep deprivation that was proving difficult to combat.

Fortunately, I had time to regain my composure as the rocks became more distant behind us and I was brought back to reality when Oscar said, "Come on Brookie, when are we going to get on with this trip, we're heading in the wrong direction!"

The squall exhausted itself and the wind swung back to a more favourable heading. I got Daisy to take a turn at the helm and we continued on our way towards Bardsey Sound, which, when we reached it, looked like the turbulent waters one would see in a washing machine. I told Daisy to keep the boat at right angles to the waves and we shot through doing about ten knots. It was like sailing across a cauldron of boiling water in a paper boat, and Daisy did a marvellous job of negotiating us safely through.

Bardsey Sound, yes, like so much of the coastline I had passed, is famous for its shipwrecks. On a map one would say it looks harmless, with a two mile gap between Bardsey Island and the Mainland. Apart from one large exposed rock that sticks up in the middle of the channel, there appears to be nothing to worry about. Bardsey's danger, however, comes from two strange tidal effects; first, that the tide in Bardsey Sound runs at a different time than the tide of the surrounding bays and, secondly, that the current does not run in exactly opposite directions on the flood and ebb, but runs east west on the flood and south east on the ebb. The fact that the water in the sound is so different from that of the local surrounds creates a maelstrom of confused waters and, as such, can easily catch out the unsuspecting sailor.

By the time we got clear of the sound, the tide was about to turn and I knew that our destination of Holyhead was not attainable in the time we had left. What do you do when the tide is against you? Go to the pub!

I had a quick look at the chart for other possible berths for the night. As the evening drew on we realized we could get to a little place called Porth Dinllaen. There's a large exposed rock at the entrance to the port and we had to do a wide circle round in the dark to spot the beacon and get into port where we picked up a mooring. I was knackered, but the others were keen to get ashore.

"Come on Brookie, we need to get to the pub," they said.

"But it's 11 o'clock at night!"

We rowed ashore and found a fabulous little pub called the Ty Coch Inn and just managed to secure a pint or two before closing time. The proprietor, Briony, and her bartender son, Stuart, welcomed us. They seemed amazed that we had turned up apparently out of nowhere in the middle of the night, in a rubber dinghy, attired in full offshore gear.

"We're just closing," they said.

"Oh, you can't do that, We've just got here," I said.

"Where have you come from?"

"We've come from Pwllheli, around Bardsey Sound."

"Bardsey Sound – What kind of boat have you got?"

"Oh, it's just a little 19 footer"

"A 19 footer! You're idiots you are. There are whirlpools and all sorts in Bardsey Sound … Right, you probably do need a drink," she said and, turning to the rest of the bar's clientele, called "Who wants to stay a bit longer?"

The rest of the population in the bar seemed quite happy to stay so she declared, "Right, we'll have a little lock-in," locked the door and poured us some well deserved beers. It was too late for food so we munched our way through some crisps and pork scratchings and I must admit I think I overdid the pork scratchings, as I had a very uncomfortable night when we got back to the boat. Rather unpleasant and not something I want to go into too much detail about …

Briony and Stuart took a great interest in our charitable fundraising, and as we departed Briony pressed a note into my hand and said, "Your story is incredible. Thank you so much for what you're doing. Here's a little present from me."

She wouldn't let me look at it and, as we rowed back in the dinghy, I didn't dare get it out of my pocket in case it blew away. It was only as we were ready for lights out back on board that Daisy and Oscar said "Come on Mike, let's have a look." I felt in my pocket and pulled out a crumpled up £50 note! How generous!

CHAPTER 11 – TOAST AND HONEY

Day 28 – 1st August – Porth Dinllaen to Holyhead

Early the next morning I made my famous porridge, which Oscar and I enjoyed, but, and this became a bit of a tradition, "As for Daisy – she's too sweet, she gets toast and honey!"

We sped out of the port and had a fantastic sail dead downwind, with the genoa goose-winged to windward. We hadn't been sailing long when we glided in awe between the sun, rising to starboard, and a magnificent rainbow on our port side. What a spectacle mother nature had put on, seemingly just for us, and it was almost as if we were being let through natures gates as a reward for all our efforts to get to our destination. We celebrated by popping up the very lively Cayman Islands Gennaker, complete with Sir Turtle, who then led us northwards to Holyhead.

The weather, however, was just a bit too good to be true and, sure enough, by the time we approached our destination, the wind was blowing Force 6 – 7 and the sails were reefed. We had to work hard using both motor and sails to make headway against the tide as we trundled round into the huge bustling port of Holyhead. Fortunately, Chal Chute had forewarned the harbour master of our arrival and we were made welcome by Geoff Garrard and his staff, Suzanne and Gweneth, who had a little spot organised for us right by the front of the marina, where we had easy access to water, showers and other facilities. What champions!

Our arrival marked the end of the fourth leg of my journey. I had now sailed nearly 400 nautical miles and was a third of the way through my adventure. Both boat and crew were in pretty good condition but I was glad I had scheduled a couple of days stopover in order to tidy and reprovision the boat, and swap crew. I was pretty knackered and hoped to get a couple of good night's kip while tied up in the safe environment of the marina.

Even on a good day my head was filled with things that had to be considered and I found myself operating in a state of relaxed tension. The stress was always there; my mind was always working, almost operating much like a multi-functioning robot, with no real emotion evident, simply calculating outside factors over and over in my mind. I don't think even I was aware of it at times as my eyes followed the clouds, calculated the windspeed, looked for gusts, squalls and other disturbances on the sea or in the sky. My ears, as

Storm clouds brewing ... again!

they listened to the chat of my crew, were, at the same time, straining for the sound of objects hitting the hull, waves breaking, things going bump or bang when they shouldn't. My voice gave instructions to the crew without thought, as I participated in a conversation, shared a story or recalled an event. My hands moved without conscious effort to tension a sheet, straighten the tiller or tighten my grip as the boat moved this way and that. Perhaps you can understand how exhausting this can be and how rare it is to find a fat person on a boat with all the energy needed for thinking, reacting and moving constantly.

DAY 29 – 2ND AUGUST - HOLYHEAD

Oscar departed the next day, after two action packed weeks on the boat, and I was sad to see him go as we had worked well together; and it's always useful to have a strong young bloke to do some of the hard physical stuff. I was certainly grateful he had been on board, when the gaff fittings failed, as I would have had a lot of problems repairing the rig without his climbing ability.

Daisy also left and I was proud to sign her Competent Crew Certificate. Yes, she left the dolphin on board, another furry crew member to add to the growing menagerie!

Goodbye good friend. Oscar Nowak in reflective mood ...

DAY 30 – 3ʳᵈ AUGUST - HOLYHEAD

While in Holyhead, the yacht club organised a fund raising evening and, once again, the locals rallied round donating prizes for the raffle. By this stage I had run out of favours with Pippa … but yes, I added a Benbow B & B prize anyway. I managed to compromise a little by making it a mid week stay rather than a weekend one, so she wasn't as cross as she might have been.

Charges waived at Holyhead Marina, many thanks

My new companion for the next leg of the voyage was a somewhat unknown quantity. David Pratt, egged on by his partner Christine, had approached me at the London Boat Show a few months earlier, wanting to be involved and to provide some support for my endeavours. Not only did he make a very generous donation but he also volunteered to crew with me from Holyhead to Port Patrick and so, true to his word, David turned up in the pouring rain.

I must apologise to him again as, at first, I didn't recognise him and thought he was a reporter from the local newspaper! David, however, is actually a judo instructor, very strong and agile, which I personally found extremely useful later in our journey, when he got me out of a rather slippery situation.

DAY 31 - 4ᵀᴴ AUGUST - HOLYHEAD TO PORT ST MARY ON THE ISLE OF MAN

David and I set sail northwards. Our first day's sailing was a fairly ambitious 45 miles across the Irish Sea to the Isle of Man, an exciting prospect, particularly as we suddenly, but fortunately, found that the wind was behind us and no baked beans were involved in this feat …

There was a huge tide round The Skerries, another nasty group of rocks just off the coast of Anglesey, and home to yet another lighthouse, this one built by a private individual with the idea of collecting a toll from all vessels that went past. While the toll collecting was not very successful, the family that owned it made a fortune when they refused to hand over ownership to the crown and were paid a huge sum of money in compensation.

The tide was so strong that, despite the Isle of Man being almost directly north of us, we were virtually pointing due west to go north! The trip was relatively quick and we made the distance in just on seven hours, almost skidding sideways for a large part of the voyage as we were pushed by the tide.

David had sailed a bit and wanted to come for the experience and get some more sailing miles under his belt. Most people would have thought that I would hug the coast when going round the country, so I think David was a little perplexed when the land disappeared off into the distance behind us and he was particularly pleased to spot the outline of the Isle of Man as it appeared over the horizon after spending quite a bit of the day on the open water with nothing solid in sight – not quite what he was expecting.

The Isle of Man is quite big with a land mass of 221 square miles, located in the middle of the Irish Sea, between Ireland and the mainland of Great Britain. Despite being smack in the middle of the UK, it is not actually part of the United Kingdom. It is a country with its own parliament, currency and tax regime. With low corporate and personal tax and no capital transfer or inheritance tax, the island has developed into a flourishing offshore business centre and is popular with tourists from the UK, who like shopping! Especially for expensive things!

Outward bound from Holyhead to Isle of Man

Drying everything out yet again!

No life raft so Avon Redstart will have to do

Theo's Future flying the flag in Port St Mary

David Pratt in the cockpit

More fund raising, more funds raised, and more beer ...

CHAPTER 12 – MANX CATS AND THREE LEGGED MEN ...

We entered Port St Mary at the south end of the island as dusk fell, and did the old trick of liberating someone's private mooring for the night ... thank you someone!

Seven hours at sea is enough to make anyone thirsty and the Albert Hotel beckoned us for a few beers. Boy, did that first pint taste good! We took the roll up stand with us and were soon chatting with the locals about our cause. As we stood in our rather haggard and dishevelled state, I was approached by Simon Tuck, a former 9/12th Lancer, and was staggered by his generosity when he offered to see what he could do to raise some money while we took ourselves off, up the road, for dinner at the local Indian restaurant. We returned a couple of hours later and, expecting a modest sum, were totally astounded when presented with a box of cash – £136.00!

Once again, the generosity of the people we met was outstanding and I felt humble and grateful that people were able to understand what I was trying to achieve and, better still, reach into their pockets for a small contribution.

Simon, however, is a military man and had a word with me as I left the pub saying "There's some more money in this for you mate. I know you're an ex-Royal Marine, and the moon's a balloon for the Royals. So, if you're prepared to drop your pants and put a photo on your website, I'll send you another 40 quid ... "

The dare was to travel with me for some time. I mean 40 quid is 40 quid. The problem was that he had made it a sum worth considering but I had to work out how to fulfil the dare in the best possible taste!

"Don't forget," he called as we disappeared into the darkness.

The next day we headed up the coast from Port St Mary to

Knackered! Cpl Simon Tuck former 9/12 Lancers taking over the evening's fundraising

Douglas, the capital of the Isle of Man. We came in through the old ferry port, up the river, and through a lock into a lovely long narrow marina, with berths at angles on each side, rather like a herringbone pattern. David and I went ashore and decided to do our own thing for the afternoon. It was pouring with rain but I strode determinedly up to the bank to hand in the cash I had collected.

Have you ever walked to a bank with a large sum of money? By this time, I had well over a thousand pounds onboard the boat so I was very conscious walking in as if I had nothing of value. The thought of it getting stolen was almost worse than the thought of getting shipwrecked and I seriously needed to offload the cash to somewhere safe. Bear in mind it was great ballast, as the amount was made up of the pennies and pounds collected from children, off old ladies and in pubs; in all, I had a very heavy and large pile of shrapnel to dispose of. Once deposited, I was certainly glad that it was safe but also relieved that I didn't have to hike around with it anymore! Some of the money collected was from the pub in Port St Mary, paid in coins from the Isle of Man, which, while still legal tender in the UK, was easier to bank on the island itself.

In Port Douglas, I also went shopping. I was thinking of Pippa as I'd been away a month and I was missing her terribly. I don't know why

With the proceeds ... £136 and another £40 to come ... maybe

Thank you Simon

but it came to mind that it would soon be our 40th wedding anniversary or, at least, it was only a few years away so, while I had some time, I wandered into a jewellers and asked to look at some ruby rings. Pip has always said she doesn't do red but I always think that ruby red is a sort of intoxicating colour and I do love a woman in red, so I got some quotes anyway. The jeweller pointed out that with its VAT levy, the Isle of Man is a good place to go shopping as you don't pay as much for some things as you would on the mainland.

I went into the next shop and I saw a very scruffy teddy bear and I thought it was so scruffy that I had to buy it. I thought that I would give it to Pip as part of my present. Then I bought a card for our anniversary as well. I must admit it was all a little premature as it was only 2008 and our 40th anniversary was still three years away. She will be pleased to know I really was missing her and was obviously keen to stay married!

Day 33 – 6th August - Douglas

Entering Douglas Harbour

Squeezed into Douglas Marina ... but free of charge – lovely job!

The next day we had a day off so thought we'd do the tourist bit and caught the steam train across the island to Port Erin for a lovely breakfast of bacon and eggs. The train was a fabulous place for fundraising and being tourist season the carriage was full and I had a captive audience. As you would expect I rustled up plenty of interest in our voyage and left the train with even more donations!

There are very few steam railways running in Britain anymore, thanks to Dr Beeching's drastic cuts in the 60s, so it was a real treat to take a train ride down on the island, so much so that we caught another train that afternoon up the mountain to the highest point on the Island at Snaefell. I don't think Dr B ever visited the Isle of Man – thank goodness! I scaled the cairn at the top of the mountain to the highest point on the island until I was the highest man

Dr Beeching never made it here!

*Douglas – Port St Mary/
Port Erin express!*

Yes it's true – amazing

Funicular railway all the way to the top

*Fund raising with total strangers on the train
journey*

Brunch in Port Erin

Laxey Wheel

On a clear day you see Scotland, England, Wales and Ireland

On top of the Isle of Man

on the Isle of Man. There was an amazing view from the summit of Ireland, Scotland, Snowdonia in Wales and England's Lake District.

Back at Douglas, the harbour master, Eric, produced a detailed passage plan to Scotland, which was of great help.

The marina didn't have a fuel dock so, later that day, I was struggling up the road in the pouring rain with the petrol cans when a car pulled up alongside and a guy called James stuck his head out.

"Who are you and what are you doing?" he asked.

"I'm Mike, I've come from the marina and I'm trying to get to a gas station so I can fill my fuel tanks," I replied.

"Right," he said, "Jump in!" and he gave me a ride to the gas station, waited while I filled the tanks, and delivered me back to the marina. Fantastic!

DAY 34 – 7ᵀᴴ AUGUST - DOUGLAS TO RAMSEY

On we went, setting off the next day for Ramsey at the northern end of the Isle of Man. We had to pass a treacherous headland at Maughold and, for once, it wasn't the wind that caused us problems but rather the fog, which made sailing more ominous and unsettling. We sailed almost silently through the fog and drizzle for most of the way, broken only by the bells on the channel markers as they dong-donged rhythmically in time with the waves when we neared our destination. While great aids to navigation, at times it is hard to work out exactly what direction the sound is coming from and one has

Poor visibility – a major threat on passage to Ramsey

to concentrate to avoid getting disoriented. Finally, we turned into Ramsey on a falling tide, in pouring rain and swirling mist. Very spooky!

We came in through the moles, round the river and as, we approached the port, I went to put fenders out when …

I lost my footing and fell over the side. Splash!

Almost a full splash but David, with the lightning fast reactions of a judo instructor, swung round, leant over the side and grabbed me by the collar, saving me from a full dunking. Not only did he grab me and stop me from falling further, but he stood up, and whipped me back up on to the deck as if I was a pillow in a pillow fight.

"No more bare feet on deck skipper," he said.

"No David," I said. "I do apologise."

I felt, as a skipper, about knee high to a grasshopper.

With my heart racing and bruises developing on my legs from where I'd bashed them as I fell, we got into Ramsey.

The harbour there is a drying harbour so we dried out and went ashore.

David wasn't feeling like an adventure but we decided to go for a wander, then meet and get some food. "Oh Mike," he said, "I want to introduce you to someone before we go," and he took me to a little shop called 'Pure Inspiration'

Ramsey's Roadbridge by night

just round the corner. The shop was interesting in that it was filled with all sorts of inspirational books and objects and was all about getting to your

96

spiritual side through all sorts of means. It had a display of rocks from the Isle of Man, which were noted for their therapeutic properties.

David said, "I know you're grieving for your son, Mike, and I've had a word with Janine, as I think she may be able to help you."

"I'm so sorry to hear of your loss," she said.

"Thank you," I replied.

"Whether you believe it or not Mike, there's a certain rock found on this island, a lovely pink colour, and it's very rare. If you rub a piece of this rock and think positively, it can ease your state of mind. I only have three pieces left, but I'm going to give you a piece because I think it will help you to deal with your loss."

I was quite taken aback at her generosity. While I am not naturally one to look for solace in such things as rocks and crystals, I took the rock and thanked her for her kindness. Strangely enough, rubbing the rock in some ways did help me to find some peace. Whether it is something to do with the power of suggestion or not, I will never know, but I still have that rock to this day, and carry it in the pocket of my sailing jacket. I was stretching a leg along the sea front when I happened upon a Roman Catholic church named 'Our Lady, Star of the Sea'. The name intrigued me and I couldn't resist poking my nose inside in case there was an opportunity to light a candle which Pippa and I often do in Chichester Cathedral in loving memory of Simon. To my delight, there were candles to be lit and, as I was lighting one or two, I noticed an inscription etched into a stone tablet on the wall behind. It was beautifully composed and I would like to share it with you:

Lord, may this candle be a light for you to enlighten me in my difficulties and decisions. May it be a fire to burn out of me all pride, selfishness and impurity. May it be a flame for you to bring warmth into my heart, towards my family, my neighbours and those who meet me along the way.

Through the prayers of Mary, Virgin and Mother, I place in your care those I come to remember, (and adding my own piece) especially Simon our dearest eldest son who is with you now. Help me to continue my prayer into everything I do this day.

I cannot stay long here with you in your church; in leaving these candles burning brightly, I wish to give you something of myself. Amen.

Needless to say, I left the stillness of the church feeling calm and somehow spiritually refreshed and more able to tackle what lay ahead on my journey of hope and endeavour.

DAY 35 – 8ᵀᴴ AUGUST - RAMSEY TO PORT PATRICK IN SCOTLAND

We left the Isle of Man on a positive note as, just as we were getting ready to depart the dock, a couple of children and their father came and asked us about the boat and what we were doing. Out came the lucky dip bag, and sure enough, we collected another donation for the cause!

Young visitor in Ramsey

CHAPTER 13 – SCOTLAND FOR THE BRAVE ...

Off we went across a lumpy open sea, heading back to the mainland on what turned out to be a very long day of sailing, so much so that we neared the coast late in the evening. As we approached Port Patrick, I had a dilemma to contend with. It was dark, and I couldn't make out the entrance to the harbour. You would think it would be lit up, and visible from miles away, and yet according to my GPS it was right in front of us, but I couldn't see anything!

The last thing I wanted was to run smack into a cliff and, looking at the chart, that's exactly what lay to either side of the entrance.

All our senses were alert for the sound of waves on rocks, a change in wind, the sight of a gap in the darkness or light on shore. Slowly we edged our way forward, with the hairs on the back of my neck standing higher and higher with each passing minute.

Suddenly, out of the darkness loomed a huge craggy shape dead in front of us. Instinctively I turned to port, evading the grasp of the rugged tendrils that reached towards us through the waves at its base. Thank God I did, as suddenly a light could be seen ahead and we realized that the harbour entrance was in fact hidden from our sight behind the giant rock we had only just avoided. Had we turned the other way our journey would have been well and truly over and we would have found ourselves in dire straits indeed.

Amazingly, nestled in behind this huge craggy cliff was a little Scottish fishing

The pure magic of dawn at sea ...

village and lifeboat station. We nudged our way into the harbour and moored up beside a large motor boat, where there was a bit of a party going on.

A door opened and a loud booming voice called, "Who are you?"

"We've just sailed up from the Isle of Man in a little boat," I replied.

"Where's your boat?"

"We're standing on it."

"Oh ... I can't see anything!"

"Well have a look."

"What! You sailed here in that?"

"Yes, We couldn't possibly moor up beside you for the night?" I asked, tentatively.

"Of course you can. Tell you what, get yourselves sorted and then come aboard for a beer."

So we had an enjoyable pint or two with our neighbours, relieved to have made it to safety for the night.

DAY 36 - 9TH AUGUST - PORT PATRICK

Constantly in touch with the weather ...

The next day, we had a day off in Port Patrick, as it was a crew changeover location. David asked if he could stay on for another leg and we were joined by Robert Goodall, the acquirer of the tracking device.

Port Patrick is in the middle of nowhere (no insult intended to the lovely locals), but my new crewmate, Robert, had to come all the way from Glasgow so ended up arriving late that afternoon. While he arrived late, he also arrived full of beans and raring to go.

"Right," he said, "What do we do to get some money out of these folks?"

"We need to find a place, put up the pop stand and whip up some enthusiasm and, hopefully, people will give. We can ask the locals if they would donate some prizes and run a raffle." I told him.

Safe and sound in Port Patrick harbour

"Well," said David, "The biggest pub is just up the road on the corner."

So off we went, sat down and had a pint.

I had a word with the landlord and asked if we could have a fundraising event that evening.

"No," he said, "No, you can't."

My heart fell as he was a very direct fellow and I thought at first he was going to be of no help at all.

"This is a tourist pub," he went on. "You don't want to do it here, you want to do it up the hill at my brother's place where the locals go. The lifeboat crew don't drink here, but they do drink up the hill at the Crown Hotel. You walk up there and I'll ring him for you."

There was no messing around, he was a busy man, slightly brusque but with a twinkle in his eye. A great Scottish lad.

Off we went up the hill where we had a great reception from his brother. "We got the message," he said, "We've got a big coach party coming in tonight to augment the locals drinking so it should be a good night. We'll organise a space for you and your stand, and you and your crew can have free beers on the house."

What else could you ask for!

I explained about running a raffle and he said, "Well, what prizes have you got?"

"I've got a mid week break at Benbow B & B for a start," I said, knowing full well that I had already used up more than the allotted three B & B prizes, but prepared to face the wrath when Pip found out. The pub donated some beers and the local lifeboat men produced some prizes from things they had left over from an event the week before including suntan lotion and other bits and bobs. I even threw in a trip around the bay on the boat.

The evening got going and there was a great crowd with plenty of frivolity as the masses imbibed and became more boisterous. The raffle tickets were selling fast.

I was mingling with some of the ladies off the coach tour and telling my story thus far. One of the them explained that her daughter ran a sports and recreation facility for the blind in Newcastle, so she suggested we give her a call when we got round there and go for a visit.

While we were having our chat, the door suddenly burst open with a huge clamour, and in walked a lady piper playing "Scotland the Brave" with great vigour, which believe me, in an enclosed space is overwhelming. The cacophony was added to by the yelling and screaming of the crowd which went wild, with old ladies standing on their chairs, clapping in time to the piper and the local blokes having a great Yahoo! The money rattled into the donation box and the publican whispered in my ear, "I hope this is OK, I couldn't rustle much up at late notice, so this was the best I could do for a Sunday night." Well, what an occasion … outstanding!

Day 37 – 10th August – Port Patrick

The next morning, I was featured in the local paper – for all the right reasons – and the town of Port Patrick helped me raise a great sum of money.

I had now done 500 miles and we had collected £24,000 already, well on our way to the target. It may seem that I had not spent much time fundraising as I sailed round the country so far, certainly not enough to raise this kind of sum. This is quite right. The fundraising had started well before I even left Bosham Quay, and many individuals had made substantial donations on hearing of our venture, including some I had never even met. While I was also collecting off the people I met as I sailed around the UK, there were groups of people in little villages dotted about holding fundraising and sponsorship events, and many of the places I visited went on to raise extra funds to support our venture after we had left, sending cheques through to 'Benbow Maritime HQ' well after we had moved on.

That day in Port Patrick, the coxswain of the lifeboat asked us to come upstairs for a moment for a serious word.

A very jolly evening's fund raising (Scottish style) with female piper

"Look," he said, "I've got you here for purely selfish reasons. You're about to tackle a particularly nasty and treacherous piece of coast, and I don't really want to have to come out and rescue you."

He got out his charts and suggested an alternative course to us. As a local he was able to give us some great advice. He was aware that our intended course around the Mull of Kintyre could put us in grave danger as our boat was small, the tides were fast and there were areas known for their whirlpools and eddies that could cause us grief in a wind over tide situation with *Theo's Future* taking advantage of the 6 hour NW tidal gate into the prevailing north-westerly – definitely NOT a happy marriage …

Instead he suggested we sail out of Port Patrick and across the Irish Sea to Glenarm on the east coast of Northern Ireland. From there we would be able to make our way north along the coast of Northern Ireland in relatively calm water and cross back again to Scotland.

DAY 38 – 11ᵀᴴ AUGUST PORT PATRICK – CARNLOUGH

So that's pretty much what we did, heading out of Port Patrick on a west norwest course on a fairly lumpy sea, which saw Robert looking a little green around the gills but he settled down with a few ginger biscuits. No sooner had we left the harbour, than David spotted a miserable semi-submerged pallet, which he avoided due to his quick thinking reactions on the helm! Such an obstacle could have damaged the hull, or at the very least broken the propeller shear pin - not something we wanted during our attempts to leave a lee shore in bumpy seas.

The miles however soon ticked off, enlivened by the sighting of two pairs of harbour porpoises. We headed for Northern Ireland where we put in for the night after five hours sailing at a tiny little harbour called Carnlough, which, rather like Port Patrick, was almost impossible to see from the sea, even in broad daylight, but absolutely delightful once we were there. The harbour was so small there was only room for ten or so boats, in fact it had to have been the smallest harbour I have ever been in my life! You could throw a rope across from one side to the other. The port was built in 1883 by the Marquis of Antrim, to export locally mined coal. High tea was taken in The Londonderry Hotel, which was once owned by Sir Winston Churchill.

We went ashore that night for a beer. Robert likes a pint or two, as does David, so Brookie the skipper wasn't going to be left out. We had a lovely

Nautical tragedy never far away ...

Grasping for life ...

Tidal retiring arch ...

steak supper and tasted several pints of the lovely black stuff from Dublin, Draught Guinness, extra cold. Fantastic!

DAY 39 – 12ᵀᴴ AUGUST CARNLOUGH TO PORT ELLEN – ISLAY

The following morning we set off again. It was a very stormy exit from the harbour due to a local weather effect, however, once out in the main channel conditions improved. *En route* we saw more harbour porpoises, a solitary puffin, and a basking shark. From Carnlough we sailed up the east coast of Northern Ireland, past Cushendun towards Rathlin Island, the northern most inhabited island of Northern Ireland and a piece of land much fought over by the Scots, English and Irish.

When we got abeam of Rathlin Island, we were able to alter course and head almost due north back across to Scotland, making for the island of Islay, famous for its whisky distilleries, where, after a full day at sea, eight hours of sailing, we arrived at Port Ellen to be welcomed by a delightful seal who was busy snacking on titbits from a local fishing boat! The pontoon had a collection of German, Norwegian and Dutch yachts tied up and we found a space among them.

Port Ellen is a delightful little town on the edge of a deep water harbour. It was founded in 1821 by Walter Frederick Campbell and named after his wife Ellinor or Eleanor, later shortened to Port Ellen. By sailing here from Northern Ireland we had avoided the Mull of Kintyre, which is a shitty place to take a little boat. If you look at a map you can see why because, the landform hangs down into the Irish Sea and compresses the sea on either side of the headland, making the tidal races very strong and creating lots of erratic currents. The area is known for the thick sea mist that rolls in across the Irish Sea and clings to the high steep craggy cliffs of the Mull or headland, which acts as the base of the obligatory lighthouse, 240 feet above the sea. While an obvious hazard to ships for centuries, the Mull has also been the site of many aeroplane crashes in later years. On a clear day however it is possible to see the coast of Ireland and, at its closest point, mainland Northern Ireland is only 12 miles away.

As it was, the trip was hard work, another one of those days when it rained constantly and the waves seemed somewhat erratic. We were out in fairly open water, in big waves with a long way to go. Not really my idea of a relaxing day's sail. I was quite relieved when we made it to our destination and, while still light, was more than ready to call it a day.

When we got safely tied up in Port Ellen, we went ashore and had a wander. I found a lovely little chapel, which was a joy, very Scottish, very plain but beautiful, and I had a little thought and said a little prayer. "Thanks Lord for getting us safely so far and long may we be able to continue. Amen." Having touched base in Northern Ireland, I was reminded of a small Irish poem about the Kinsale Hooker, a nineteenth century fishing vessel, not the type you may be thinking about!

The Kinsale Hooker
"His hooker's in the Scilly Van, when seines are in the foam;
But money never made the man, nor wealth a happy home.
So, bless'd with love and liberty, while he can trim a sail;
He'll trust in God, and cling to me, the boatman of Kinsale."
                    Thomas Osbourne Davies 1815-1845

Despite the incessant pouring rain, the evening was spent in the local Indian curry house in Port Ellen and, having acquired a bottle of red from the Co-op down the road, we could probably have been accused of not supporting the local industry!

The Port Pantry, Portpatrick. ©Mark & Karen Bevan, by kind permission

CHAPTER 14 – THE SOUNDS OF SILENCE ...

Day 40 - 13ᵀᴴ August Port Ellen to Crinan

The next day conditions were much calmer. We still had to take a lot of care navigating around the craggy coastline and planned to head a mile or so out to sea to avoid the numerous rocks and islets that were dotted up the coast of the island. Out of the shelter of the harbour and around on the more exposed coastline of the island, we had another tricky escape from a lee shore with a scrap of staysail and outboard motor working hard in a rough onshore chop. We were definitely relieved to leave the last set of jagged exposed rocks behind us and we made for deeper water to avoid any more of the deadly creatures hiding beneath the surface of the sea.

Once we were past the headland at Kintour we were in more open water and made fairly steady but slow progress, sailing into a headwind northeast up the Sound of Jura towards mainland Scotland. It seemed to take hours to pass the huge long hilly island of Jura, on our left, and head across the Sound to Crinan, which is at the mouth of the Crinan Canal. I had been intending to use this canal to cross from Ardrishaig on the other side of the Kintyre peninsula but had earlier heard there was a blockage part way along as one of the locks was not working. Had the canal been operational, the sailing would have been somewhat easier as I could have left Port Patrick and sailed into the Firth of Clyde, cutting out many miles of open sea, and our visit to Northern Ireland which, as it turned out, would have been a pity.

My friend Dick Pratt's daughter-in-law's sister (work that out for yourselves) lived half way along this canal and, though we hadn't been able to cruise right past their front door as

More storm clouds brewing together with a brief glimpse of the Gulf of Corryvreckan, dangerous currents and whirlpools, looks peaceful but definitely to be avoided.

Aerial view of Port Ellen

Across the bay to the Fisherman's Chapel.
© H J Underwood, Isle of Islay, by kind permission

Kate, Richard, Imogen and Finley
at the Crinan Canal

I had hoped, we had organised to see them. We anchored at Crinan, went ashore for beers, gave her a ring and, sure enough, Kate Moody with her two delightful children, Finley and Imogen, came and got us, as well as all our dirty laundry. We drove back to her house, which she and her husband Richard were restoring and which is situated virtually on the canal in a magical setting. We had hot showers and a wonderful evening, waking the next morning to a huge Scottish breakfast complete with black pudding. Finley showed me the tracking system for the first time on his computer and I was amazed to think of how so many people were able to remotely track my progress hour by hour. We felt a million dollars by the time Kate drove us back to the boat, complete with full tummies, clean clothes and having had a good night's sleep.

DAY 41 – 14TH AUGUST CRINAN TO OBAN

We climbed aboard and headed out of Crinan, turned to starboard and set sail for Oban past numerous beautiful scenic headlands that disappeared into the distance as we made our way north through the

Facing page:
Moored at Crinan in the dawn.

© David Pratt

tangle of little islands, rocks and land masses. We were in high spirits and had a magnificent day, sailing through what could have been lethal stretches of water but, on this particular day, with the tide and wind co-operating, we were able to make safe and speedy progress without great effort.

Oban itself is a busy little port, previously used for shipping whisky, kelp, wool and slate to other parts of Great Britain but now bustling with ferries that run to many of the outer Outer Isles, earning the town its title of "The Gateway to the Isles".

In Oban, we once again handed over some money to the bank as I was very conscious now of carrying large sums of money and we had a fair pile, especially after the fantastic fundraising evening in Port Patrick, which raised over £300!

DAY 42 – 15ᵀᴴ AUGUST – OBAN TO FORT WILLIAM

Keeping to our routine, we started our morning with a good hot bowl of porridge and a cup of tea before heading off to Fort William, further north at the top of Loch Linnhe. This leg of the journey was very tricky, with lots of craggy rocks to negotiate, and we sailed northwest out of Oban towards the Isle of Mull. On one of the rocky hilltops we could see Duart Castle, home to the MacLean Clan, guarding the Sound of Mull. We turned on a more northerly course at the bottom of Lismore Island. While nearly ten miles long, the island is only just over a mile wide and is a remote and sparsely populated landform, with mottled blocks of green fields stretching down to the rocky shoreline.

At one point, we came round a small headland and had to take evasive action as there was a partially submerged rock right in front of us. It wasn't on the chart and it was lucky I had noticed the white wash as the water swept over the rock, which was lurking just below the surface of the water, ready to catch us out. It was a great reminder to me that this part of the coast is sparsely populated and very few but the locals sailed here. The charts were also perhaps not as detailed as they could be and one had to be constantly alert for hidden dangers such as the one we almost encountered. Were we to run into difficulty, help would take a while to arrive, and should we make it to shore it would be a long way to civilization to get assistance. I would not like to be caught out on this stretch of water after dark.

Past the rolling green hills of Lismore Island we continued up Loch Linnhe, and maintained a pretty straight course towards Fort William. With the wind behind us, we were able to fly the gennaker once more. The scenery was spectacular and I realised that very few indeed would have had the pleasure of sailing this course. There is something about the hues and colours of the Scottish mountains that are quite different from England. The mauve of the heather and the low sun with its gold light seems to enrich the normally drab browns of the bracken and gorse and create instead a rich tapestry, reflected in the still waters around the edges of the loch. I imagine anyone watching us would have thought the scene, with our little boat and its colourful Sir Turtle Gennaker were postcard material.

As we neared Fort William we almost sailed through a fleet of little dinghies having an evening race, an impromptu rendezvous with the local sailing club, so we knew we were near our destination. We whipped the sails down as we went through and motored back towards the club and picked up one of their buoys. A rescue rib came out to see us and we explained what we were doing and asked if we were able to use their mooring for the night.

"Of course you can," Jim Shearer, the Vice Commodore of the local yacht club, replied, followed by an invitation to come over to the club for a pint or two. We joined the dinghy sailors, swapped some stories over a few beers and then it was time for the club to pack up.

"Tell you what," they said, "We'll give you a ride down into Fort William, but you'll have to catch the bus back. The last bus leaves at 10.30 so don't miss it and, by the way," he said, throwing some keys on the table, "Here are the keys to the clubhouse, so you can come back and use the showers."

How thoughtful! We thanked him and expressed our delight at the fabulous new facilities they had.

"We had a fire a while ago," explained Jim, "and our clubhouse burnt down, so this is our new clubhouse. In the old clubhouse we had burgees from clubs all round the country displayed around the walls of the clubroom. It was a real shame when we lost the lot."

I was quite moved and said, "Your kindness means I'm going to get my club burgee for you."

I couldn't help the bitter memory of the Bosham Sailing Club Commodore's comments about the sailing club not being able to support me as I lowered my flags and removed the Bosham Sailing Club Burgee, which I took ashore and gave to the club members to help with their collection.

I'm sure the sailing club would still appreciate any burgees, so anyone reading this who would like to contribute a burgee to the club can contact them: Lochaber Yacht Club, Achintore Road, Fort William PH33 6RN Scotland.

So, in we went to Fort William and Robert, in fine fettle and with a rather insatiable appetite for beer, soon had us firmly ensconced in one of the local taverns. It was his last night on board and as we weren't sailing anywhere the next day, he saw no reason to hold back on the beverages. We only just made the bus back to the clubhouse and God only knows how we managed to row back to the boat without getting wet. The thought crossed my mind how irresponsible we were and how many stupid people drown when they've drunk too much. Alcohol and dinghies just don't work.

Day 43 – 16th August – Corpach

Next morning we went to the clubhouse only to find that someone had beaten us to it and left us some fresh bread, eggs and bits and pieces for our breakfast. How amazing! Once again I was overwhelmed with the kindness of these people who had taken us to their hearts, instantly placing their trust in us, providing us with great company, the use of their clubhouse, food and hot showers. I had already made so many new friends on this journey and, time and again, had been taken aback by the kindness of strangers. In a world of scepticism and suspicion, it is heartening to know that the good of mankind hasn't disappeared and, in fact, thrives, surprisingly appearing from the most unexpected quarters.

What more could a seafarer ask for?

We tidied up our mess and left in fine spirits, taking the clubhouse key with us, with instructions for me to drop it with the lockmaster at Corpach, my next port of call at the start of the Caledonian Canal.

It was time for both my companions to leave. We had been through a lot together and there were big hugs all round. Robert and David presented *Theo's Future* with a puffin for luck, another addition to the onboard menagerie. Off they set together to the Fort William train station, heading back to civilization to resume their normal lives once more.

For me, normality was somewhat skewed, my world consisted of a 19 foot boat, a limited area to move around, little time for anything but sailing, checking the course, making food, checking the course again, sorting the provisions, checking the course again and with luck making port at the end of a day for a cooked supper, hopefully a pint, some fundraising, then back to the boat to check the course one more time before bed. I couldn't remember the last time I had sat and read the paper, gone for a leisurely stroll, or indeed been on my own for more than an hour at a time. While I am not by nature a solitary man, one does get extremely tired of always being enthusiastic, putting on a brave face and being calm in what I know to be quite dangerous situations.

With their departure I plopped myself down in the cockpit of the boat, suddenly exhausted, both physically and mentally. For the first time in days I was on my own and I sat there for a few moments, letting the tide of weariness ebb away.

The sun was shining, so I gathered my wits ready to continue on my way. I started the outboard engine and, first go, it roared into life. I dropped the mooring and motored up round the bend in Loch Eil to Corpach and prepared to come alongside a small pontoon just outside the huge lock gates at the start of the Caledonian Canal. For once I was alone and had to go through the mental checklist of everything that had to be prepared before I tied up alongside. Fenders out, bow and stern lines in reach and ready to throw. I took it slowly as I was on my own, gently nudged the boat up against the pontoon and tied up waiting for the lock to open. There were no signs of life so I climbed the ladder and went up to the lock keepers office. The sea lock is tidal, so the lock can only be opened when the tide is right. As luck would have it the lock keeper arrived when needed, so I introduced myself and handed him the key to the Sailing Clubhouse at Lochaber Yacht Club. *"Oh,"* he said, "I know all about you. Chaloner Chute has been in touch and we have everything organised for you."

He gave me my tickets and maps and arranged for me to tie up alongside a larger yacht suggesting that I join this yacht in going through the lock at the same time. My boat was only small and the amount of water flowing through the lock was very powerful, not a good combination, and I didn't want to damage the boat by getting washed against the concrete walls. I would be going through with a larger yacht, in this case *Driftwood* owned by the RAF. Originally from Lossiemouth on the north east coast of Scotland, the yacht was returning from an adventure training exercise, and the lads on board were more than happy for me to accompany them. I was very grateful as the larger boat deflected much of the impact from the water as the lock filled, which was great.

I stayed with this yacht for the first two locks and spent the first night at the quayside of Corpach town itself, which is just a little further inland.

The Caledonian Canal is 62 miles long, running between Fort William (Corpach) and Inverness. While man-made for about a third of the way, it also incorporates Loch Dochfour, Loch Ness, Loch Oich and Loch Lochy. There are 29 locks, four aqueducts, and 10 bridges in the course of the canal. It can accommodate ships up to 36 feet wide and is at least 18 feet deep. Opened in 1822, it has been a major waterway connecting the north east of Scotland to the south west, allowing ships to avoid the lengthy and dangerous route around the north coast via Cape Wrath and the Pentland Firth.

Finally entering the Caledonian Canal sea lock

CHAPTER 15 – GETTING SHIPSHAPE …

DAY 44 – 17ᵀᴴ AUGUST – CORPACH TO BANAVIE

Next morning I made my way up through three more locks to Banavie, a town that lies at the bottom of Neptune's Staircase. Neptune's Staircase is made up of eight locks that are hydraulically operated and raise a boat in total over the eight locks by a total of 64 feet (19.5 m). I carried on to the base of the Staircase and, when I inquired about where I could tie up, was told to keep going up the Staircase and there would be plenty of excellent places to tie up alongside the canal at the top.

From there I would be able to walk down into Fort William, or catch a bus to the Spean Bridge Commando Memorial, which was a special shrine that I wanted to visit.

As I went through the locks I sat in the cockpit thinking; "Wow, what an amazing week." I didn't actually regret being on my own.

Pippa was joining me on the evening of the 20ᵗʰ and it was now the afternoon of the 17ᵗʰ so while sleeping for three days was an inviting option, in fact I had a few days up my sleeve to go over the boat with a fine tooth comb. I wanted to strip it out completely and put it back together. I wanted to check everything. Check the skin fittings, check the integrity of the hull, check for leaks, though I think we'd already dealt with those along the way, and also check the sails as I knew I had a few small mending jobs to do.

I've always enjoyed sewing and it's an extraordinary thing, as sewing is usually associated with girls, but sailors have historically had to be good at sewing. Using big needles and big thread, and driving the needle through sailcloth takes quite a bit of effort, which is a man's job really, so I was quite looking forward to stitching the small rip I had found in the mainsail.

Piggy backing with the RAF, Theo's Future too small to get through on her own

I also wanted to explore the area around Fort William. Just to the north is the Spean Bridge Memorial, a special monument built in honour of the WWII Army Commandos, and I thought I'd walk there, commando style. As a Royal Marine Commando myself, I couldn't possibly take a bus. If the boys could get up Ben Nevis and back before breakfast, I could surely simply walk a couple of miles to the memorial. So I really had quite a bit to fill the

Neptune's Staircase ... seven locks

two or three days before Pip arrived and I was glad, as I didn't want to sit around doing nothing – at least not all day!

As is often the way, the weather packed in by the afternoon and, as the barometer dropped, so too did my heart sink, and I found myself feeling rather miserable and tired about how I was supposed to get everything clean, dry, mended and aired, with the weather the way it was, and only a few days 'till my next most important guest was to appear.

Some good news, however, lifted my spirits as I spoke on the phone to Annu Mayor at Fight for Sight and learned that our fundraising target of £27,500 had just been reached!! WOW, WOW, WOW!!!

Ben Ainslie may have won his 3rd gold medal the day before at the Bejing Olympics but *Theo's Future* had won its own very special 'Gold' that very day too and I felt incredibly grateful for everyone's support.

Rousing myself, despite the pouring rain, I went ashore to try

Made it to the top

and find a computer to use to write my blog, which I was rather late in sending. I had a longhand version but needed somewhere to type it out. Alongside Neptune's Staircase is a real one, interspersed with sections of pathway for people to climb up and down beside the lock system. About half way down the Staircase, I passed a lovely hotel called The Moorings and went in to cheekily ask if I could use a computer. I must have looked like a bedraggled rat or a vagrant, as I stood there dripping, but Frances at reception took pity on me and asked me in. While it was not normally allowed, she also let me use her computer to type and email my blog. We chatted, as I worked, and I told her my story.

In the corner was a man sitting in a chair and I assumed he was an employee of some kind but, after I had finished, he spoke to me and said, "Mike," he said, "I'm Stuart Leitch, I own the hotel and I'm staggered to hear your story."

"Oh God," I thought, "Here I am, looking like a tramp, getting the receptionist to break the rules, hope he doesn't call the police!"

He beckoned to the young lady at the reception desk and said, "I think, um, room number seven is free tonight."

"So Mike," he said, "Have a night here on us, there's the key … bed and breakfast is on us."

Someone upstairs must have really been looking out for me, and how surprising because seven is my lucky number! Ignoring the rain, I trotted to the boat to get some washing gear and clean clothes, returning to the hotel to make the most of their hospitality. I had been living pretty much in a sleeping bag, so this was luxury. The hotel was very upmarket and upon entering room number seven, I took off my shoes and found my feet sinking into deep pile carpet. It felt very odd indeed!

I normally tried to stay on the boat, but just every now and then, when the opportunity was offered, I succumbed. Here, for the third time in my journey, I fell asleep in the bath. The problem with falling asleep in the bath is you wake because you and the water are cold. I must have been in the bathroom for over two hours! I had a hot shower to warm myself up again, got dressed and went downstairs for some supper.

DAY 45 – 18TH AUGUST – BANAVIE

After a great night's sleep, another long hot shower and a fantastic Scottish breakfast with all the trimmings I went back to the boat the next morning. The action man in me was feeling revived and it was time to get on with things.

It was now the 18th, so I had a busy day getting some of my tasks done, mending sails and sorting out the boat. The weather improved again so I was able to get things dry and aired. I was somewhat distracted however during my day's work as, within sight, was a delightful little pub, which sold lovely cold draught Guinness. I could hear Pip in my head saying *"Come on Brookie, work first. No drinking. Set yourself some tasks and get them done. Then you can have a drink."* So I made myself a list of tasks to complete before I was allowed to go to the pub for a pint or two. Pip would have been proud of me. Rest assured though, by the end of the day, I had made friends with the pub!

DAY 46 – 19TH AUGUST – BANAVIE

The next day, I set out to visit the Spean Bridge Memorial and took the bus to the bottom of the valley as, being an ex Royal Marine Commando, I really had to get there under my own steam. I have to admit I was pretty knackered by the time I had climbed the hill but I was glad I had made the effort as it was the most incredible place to visit.

There is a commemorative garden near the memorial where anyone who's lost a loved one can leave a flower, a poppy, a cross or some memento. It was fascinating to see that families had left a token with their son, or uncle, or nephew's name and unit on it, and then another family had seen it, and because

Spean Bridge Commando Memorial

WWII Commando Marching Boot!

118

their loved one was from the same unit, they've left their token beside the other. It may be that at some future memorial they may meet and share their experiences because, as I know, death is grim but talking about it with others who have had to endure similar losses is healing.

Commando Memorial Garden at Spean Bridge for fallen comrades, Gulf War, Iraq, Afghanistan, what next …

DAY 47 – 20TH AUGUST – BANAVIE

On the 20th I finished cleaning and tidying the boat, having got rid of the rather noxious fug of wet weather gear and dirty socks that had pervaded the interior over the last few weeks. No stone was left unturned to eradicate the male smells in favour of sweet odours for Mrs B! I loaded up with yummy rations and walked down to meet Pip off the bus from Glasgow at the Fort William coach station. It was brilliant to see her after 46 days apart. I didn't tell her but I carried a special message from her on *Theo's Future* – here it is:

To You, Just Because ...
You're very
Special
 To me
I want this to put
a smile on your face.
I want it to tell you that
I think you're wonderful.
I want it to help you remember
... every time you see it
In days yet to be ...
That this was given to you ...
Just because you're very special to me.

From Pippa to Mike

"Jacobite" nearly ran me over
at Corpach Junction ...

CHAPTER 16 – THERE BE MONSTERS …

DAY 48 – 21ST AUGUST – BANAVIE TO FORT AUGUSTUS

Next day, we set off motoring up the canal. As we proceeded, I had an inkling that the weather may be changing. I looked up and thought, "Uh oh, it's a bit too bright, a bit too clear, a bit too nice, a warm front, hello, we're in Scotland!" The wind was rising and I was hoping it would be favourable for us. The wind in this area tends to get channelled between the hills and blows one of two ways, either up the loch or down the loch. The direction could make a huge difference to the length of the journey and the enjoyment of the experience.

We carried on under motor up the canal, having a lovely time, went through the two locks at Gairlochy and stopped for a lovely cup of much needed coffee.

We pushed away from the canal edge and came round the bend in the canal however into the face of a howling gale, force six blowing straight down Loch Lochy toward us. On the nose! "Oh shit," I thought. The white caps of the waves were moving towards us like an entire army of white plumed riders on horseback. This was not going to be fun.

Pip suggested we went back and waited for the weather to change, but, put simply, I couldn't afford to waste a day as I had other commitments that I needed to meet further on. "Next thing you know," said Pip, "You'll be wanting to put a sail up."

"Oh dear," I thought, "This isn't going well."

I explained that the little 5 hp engine wouldn't be able to make any headway on its own and that we would have to beat up the loch if we were to make any progress.

"Come on," I said, "Let's knuckle down, oilskins on, get nice and warm and just do it and get to the other end."

Fort Augustus, locking through …

"We haven't got much choice darling, have we?" she said.

"No," I replied, "but I think that's the best we can do."

"You so and so," She protested, "You dragged me up here to Scotland, to come sailing, to go on a canal, and now, we're facing a near gale up a lousy loch."

"No darling, it's a beautiful loch!"

"No it's not, it's a lousy loch! Get on with it then ..."

Up the Caledonian with Pippa – together again hooray!

So off we set and my heart sank because I wanted more than anything for her to have a good time, and I'd promised her lovely sailing and canals. There we were with no one else to be seen, just a few birds that one could imagine were laughing at us. Anyone with any brains had already gone to the pub. We were on our own.

We finally reached the end of Loch Lochy after about three and a half hours. The boat was soaked, Pip was soaked and we hadn't spoken for quite some time. I thought she was going to give me another roasting and demand that she go home.

Just then the sun peeped out and Pip looked up and absolutely astounded me by saying, "If this is a half, no, a fraction of what you've had to put up with up the western coast of Britain, then I think I have a better understanding of what you've been through."

It was my turn to be gobsmacked. What a lovely thing to say! She had reached a point of understanding and it was almost as if the Good Lord had given her a taste of it so she could understand the size of the challenge. We were in no danger, it was just a shitty, breezy, spumey sail for three and a half hours, which I actually absolutely adored, but I wasn't going to tell her that!

We went through the lock at Laggan and Pip said, "I want to stop now, I've had enough!"

"Oh," I said, "Look, we've just got Loch Oich to do."

"Not another loch!" cried Pip.

"Look, let's keep going. We can get through Loch Oich, which is very narrow and not very long. The weather's improved, so let's get ourselves up to Fort Augustus and we can have a proper supper and a proper stopover."

So with only a modest amount of grumbling from the crew, we carried on about a mile and a half up the canal, under a swing bridge and into Loch Oich. We didn't even bother sailing, but motored across in about an hour and made it into the next canal.

There we were, sitting at the bottom of the next lock at Culloch waiting for the water to fill, when I heard a yell, "Oy, get back here, you'll fall in."

A little child was peaking over the edge of the lock looking at our boat. She was fascinated by the streamers and flags, which I had put up to dry. "Look," she said to someone behind her, "It's a pretty boat!"

As the water filled, we were gradually able to see each other and have a little chat. Once more I got out my lucky dip bag and asked if she wanted to get something out of the bag. "Ooh, yes!" she said. I asked her the question about the lifeboat, and admittedly she was probably too little to know the answer. I made certain, however, throughout my voyage, that not one child failed this test, as I would coach them through what a lifeboat was. "Mummy, mummy, look at my teddy bear keyring," she cried when she had succeeded.

The mum dutifully arrived looking sceptically at me, and you could see her thinking, "Grubby old man chatting to children."

I explained politely that I was sailing round Britain to raise money that might help my godson who was blind and … you guessed it … sure enough … twenty quid. Net profit £16.50. Thank you very much!

On we went up the canal and, much to Pip's relief, finally made it to Fort Augustus. Pippa's relief turned somewhat to dismay when we got there, as there were no showers available and she would have loved to wash her hair. My offer of a bucket for the exercise was promptly turned down. Fortunately Pippa is much better on the water than she thinks she is and, despite liking her creature comforts, she's more than capable of surviving when push comes to shove.

We went ashore and found somewhere to eat and have a few drinks, so the day ended well. We ate well, drank well and fell into bed.

DAY 49 – 22ND AUGUST – FORT AUGUSTUS TO TOMNAHURICH

Waking the next morning after a refreshing night's sleep, we were both pleased to be greeted by clear skies and little wind. I was particularly relieved, as I wasn't sure how a repeat performance of the day before might go down.

But what was ahead of us?

Another bloody great loch!

Thank God it was calm or I think I may not have had a crew.

Loch Ness is known for its "Ripples Unconfirmed," indicating that something might be lurking below the surface …

Loch Ness – ripples unconfirmed …

I think Pip was feeling a bit nervous about it and she stated, "Right Brookie. I'm calling the shots today."

"No you're not. I'm the boss of this boat!"

"No, you're bloody well not the boss today. Yesterday you got me wet and I had a miserable time, so today I'm in charge and we're going to motor non-stop, flat out from A to B."

"Oh, but I wanted to stop and go to the Loch Ness museum …"

"No," she declared, "You're not going there. You're not doing any of that. You're not doing anything at all except getting from A to effing B."

"All right Darling, if that's what your wish, then that is what we shall do," and we set off motoring up the Loch.

Half way across Loch Ness, Pippa glanced down at the outboard motor and noticed that the stainless steel bracket that held the engine to the boat was almost sheared through on one side and starting to go on

Fort Augustus with floral tributes to Nessy

the other. If that gave way, not only would the engine plunge to the depths of Loch Ness to stir the waters of the local beastie, but it could do a lot of damage to the back of the boat as it went. I told Pip what I had found and stopped the boat. Pip was obviously concerned, but also let me know that despite having engine problems it was no excuse for going to the museum!

When needs must, joking aside, she realised we had to solve this and did everything she could to help.

I got a lashing from the front of the engine through the D-ring in the cockpit and used a piece of wood to make a Spanish windlass to tension it. I also added another lashing from the first to the floor of the cockpit to keep the engine at the right angle.

We were able to get going again and were in no real danger of losing the engine, but I realised we would have to do something about it pretty promptly.

So, on we motored the rest of the way straight up Loch Ness and I didn't get to go to the museum.

We got up to Dockalich and Pip made a dash ashore for the local loos, returning much relieved, and we had a cup of tea.

While there I rang Bob Brown, from Honnor Marine, and explained the situation. I was half expecting a disgruntled reception but Bob couldn't have been more helpful and arranged to courier a replacement bracket to Inverness to arrive there the next day. I was able to give him an address for our friends Colin and Carol Gilmour, who we were planning to link up with in Inverness. He assured me it would leave immediately and we briefly discussed ideas for redesigning the offending piece so as to make improvements for future boats. "Just in case this post thing doesn't work I'll get the old one welded in a boat yard," I told Bob.

"Fine," he said, "keep the receipt and we'll fix you up when you get back." As it later turned out, Scott Anderson and the staff at

Pippa suddenly spotted the fractured outboard motor bracket ... horror

Improvised solution until repaired by S/S Welders at Caley Boat yard. Well done and thank you

Caley Marina in Inverness couldn't have been more helpful and did a magnificent stainless steel welding job. The new one did arrive so I was well set up for the rest of the journey. I suppose in some ways I had pushed the limits that the boat was designed for and it was possibly a case of a little boat being asked to do more than it was designed to do.

Feeling much better for having a solution in process, we carried on. There we were back in the canal system, chugging along under motor and heading for Tomnahurich, where a large swing bridge controls the road traffic and movement of boats on the canal. I knew we had to book a time to get the swing bridge opened

Loch Ness and Castle Urquhart

so we pulled up alongside the canal wall and went to the local information centre to ring and make a booking. As we had arrived late in the afternoon, we were told that the bridge would not be opening until early the following morning so we spent the night there, making use of the rations we had on board … 'Spag Bog' and a bottle of wine.

DAY 50 – 23ʳᵈ AUGUST – TOMNAHURICH TO INVERNESS

After motoring the short distance up the canal and through the lock system next morning, we parked the boat in the marina in Inverness, where we were met by Carol and Colin. We drove with them to their lovely home at

Shenaval, which is in fact like a miniature castle that they have been slowly restoring since Colin left the army.

"We've put the extra hot water on for you so you can have a lovely hot bath," said Carol.

"Oh," I said, "Baths have a rather soporific effect on me, I might fall asleep …"

"No danger of that," said Carol, "The smell of my cooking will wake you up!"

As it turned out there was no danger of

Pippa trying to keep out the way … no hiding place on Theo's Future!

me falling asleep as Pip was very keen to get in the bath after me and I got the 'hurry up' call to get out.

We had a lovely couple of evenings with Carol and Colin, and Carol dropped us back to the boat so Pip and I could get some work done.

Pip was leaving the next day and I had new crew arriving so much of the day was spent sorting out the engine bracket and restoring order to the boat in preparation for the next leg of the voyage. We had a nice supper and stayed aboard the boat that night.

Greeted by Colin and Carol Gilmour at Inverness Marina

DAY 52 – 25ᵀᴴ AUGUST – INVERNESS

Carol very kindly arrived to take Pip to the airport the next day and I must admit to having a bit of a cry when I said goodbye to her. I was going to miss her dreadfully and, for a while, my heart was quite low. For all the drama of the first day we had had a lovely time and I knew I had several more difficult weeks ahead of me before I saw her again. Almost 1000 nautical miles done and we enter the North Sea tomorrow.

I didn't however have long to feel sorry for myself as I was soon joined by my new crew members, a pair of babes - Georgina Peters and Laura Fulton known as "Fully." These two knew each other from Aberdeen University so were the best of mates. Fully is now a consultant anaesthetist and a fabulously brainy woman, with a broad Scottish accent. The pair had earlier sailed with me, Georgina's father Richard, Pat Clarke and my son James across the Atlantic in *Never Look Back*.

Georgina arrived first and we had to wait for Laura as she was unable to escape hospital duties until Monday night. We met her at the station and celebrated the reformation of half the Atlantic Rally for Cruisers (known as the ARC) team in a lovely local Scottish pub complete with "Highland PT" and haggis!

SCOTT SH LASSES

New crew at Inverness – a pair of Scottish Lasses!
Laura Fulton and Georgina Peters

© Scottish Heritage
reproduced by kind permission

Day 53 – 26th August – Inverness to Lossiemouth

We departed Inverness in light weather and made our way out of the top sea lock of the Caledonian Canal and under the huge Kessock Bridge into the Moray Firth, spotting a seal on the way. There wasn't much wind so we motor sailed eastward on what can only be described as a typically murky Scottish day. George (as she is often referred to!) cooked a wonderful breakfast and we were soon on our way past historic Fort George where one of the Highland regiments is still based. It was with some relief that we heard rifle fire after we had sailed passed … oops we must have sailed through the range danger area by mistake. Rap on the knuckles for Colonel Brookie!

We carried on along the miles and miles of sandy coastline and picked up a bit of breeze just past Nairn so had a lovely sail past the sandbanks of Findhorn, round Burghead, along the coast past Lossiemouth headland and into the Lossiemouth harbour. A much better first day for my new crew than Pip's experience.

It was here that I caught up with some of my previous companions. The RAF yacht *Driftwood* that had shepherded me through the first couple of lochs on the Caledonian Canal was based in Lossiemouth. I had arranged to ring Nigel Hessing, the skipper, when we arrived as the boys on the yacht had promised to look after us when we got to town. No doubt having a couple of lovely girls on board would be appreciated.

No sooner had we got into the little harbour than Nigel arrived to get us. Standing at the top of the steps he called, "Hello, remember me? Get yourselves sorted and sign in with the harbour master so we can get going. I've got a surprise for you."

Well the girls had never seen this man before in their lives and were not at all sure about what to expect. Their trepidation increased when he called

"Bring your toothbrush and your nighties girls."

"You'd better look after us," said the girls looking at me somewhat anxiously.

"Look, I got you safely across the Atlantic. It'll be all right and I'll never be more than a stone's throw away from you," I reassured them.

So we all got in his silver five series BMW and away we sped out of Lossiemouth and further into the wilds beyond. I must admit that, when we turned into a forest road, even I was beginning to wonder what he had in store for us.

Suddenly, we were in a clearing and, rather like in a fairy tale, we stopped outside a quaint little cottage. One had to wonder what we would find inside, either a wicked witch or the three bears?

"Right," he said, "Make yourselves at home. Have a bath – I'm off to get curry!"

Wow! What were we going to do?

"Look," I said, "You girls have a shower, I'll hike back to that little shop we passed and get some supplies."

I returned later laden with a couple of bottles of wine and some chocolates, only to find I couldn't get in! The door was locked and I had to go round and bang on the window so the girls could hear me over the noise of the stereo, which they now had blasting through the house.

"Come on girls, you've only known the man a few minutes and you've already gone through his cupboards!" I got the impression that they had taken his instruction to make themselves at home to heart.

The house smelt vaguely fruity, of feminine perfumes, and there were clouds of steam and suds still dissolving in the bathroom when I went to get clean.

Nigel arrived back with bags of takeaway curries steaming hot and spreading delectable fragrances through the air. "I thought you lot were Royal Engineers. Why haven't you got the fire going?" he declared. Within moments he had a crackling blaze in the fireplace and we sat in the kitchen contentedly eating the fabulous meal he had bought for us.

"Right," he said, "Let's get round the fire and play Monopoly!"

How surreal. None of us expected this. We sat and played Monopoly, drinking wine and munching Cadbury chocolates.

"None of us is going anywhere," Nigel declared later. "You girls can share a double bed, my room's down the hall and if you don't mind Mike, I have a mattress you can sleep on in the lounge." We all got sorted and I'm sure I would have fallen straight to sleep but the girls kept giggling in the room next door and I had to tell them to shut up!

Babes in the wood! Choccy time …

Approaching Lossiemouth

With our host, Nigel Hessing, at his country cottage

CHAPTER 17 – WHALE OF A TIME …

DAY 54 – 27ᵀᴴ AUGUST – LOSSIEMOUTH TO GARDENSTOWN

Next morning we had breakfast together and Nigel dropped us back into town on his way to work. "Remember the light blue of the RAF rules," he said as he left. What a wonderful welcome he had given us!

We got back to the boat and found to our surprise, a crate of fresh veggies and a tray of eggs, with a note from Chief Tech Tam McKeown, one of the other crew I had met off the boat. With it was a note saying he was sorry he had missed us and hoped we would appreciate the bits and bobs he and a couple of the other locals had put together for us. Once again, I was astounded by the generosity of the people we met throughout the voyage.

We signed off with the harbour master, and sailed away in moderate breezes bound for Gardenstown, home of the Cetacean Research and Rescue Unit (a small but very special charity), where my friend Dr Kevin Robinson was based, working with students in studying the local marine life.

We had another great day's sailing, and we made good time across Spey Bay towards our destination. The coastline slowly became more rugged as the long sandy beaches gave way to rocky bays and craggy outcrops. The girls made sandwiches and salad from the crate of food for lunch and we sat, watching the coast glide by. I was particularly grateful that the conditions were manageable as this part of the North Sea is not the place to be out sailing in when storms are brewing. We covered a lot of ground or, perhaps more correctly, water that day and I was pleased to see the miles go by across the top of the country as it meant it wouldn't be long before I turned south on the homeward stretch

We rounded the corner of a huge smelly rock, covered with roosting shags,

Hooray, Hooray, approaching the tiny harbour of Gardenstown home of the Cetacean Research and Rescue Unit (CRRU)

*Big hugs with Kev, Dr Kevin Robinson,
Chief Executive of CRRU*

Cheeky pair!

crossed the bay and entered the tiny harbour at Gardenstown, a small fishing village clinging to terraced ledges on the steep hills surrounding Gamrie Bay. There, standing on the high harbour wall, was Kevin. What a legend! He looked just the same as when I last saw him, with his long mop of blond hair and a big smile. We had big hugs and went ashore to his house to sort out sleeping arrangements before heading out for a pub supper. Kevin told me to have his bed, Georgina and Laura shared another room and he was going to camp somewhere else. That was fine and we went off to dinner.

Big emotional link up …

On our return, we went to bed and I got in to Kevin's bed and, twice as quickly, got out again. What on earth?!

I turned the light on and found the bed was full of cornflakes! Not only that, but I could only put my feet in half way.

Someone had apple-pied the bed …

I let out a yelp and Kevin came to find out what was the matter.

"So sorry about that," said Kevin, "It must have been my last lot of students, there were a few that were up for just about anything. We can sort it out."

So in the middle of the night, after a few drinks at the pub, I was remaking the bed.

"What shall we do with these?" I said pointing to the pile of cornflakes in the middle of the sheet.

"Oh, just put them back in the packet, we can have them for breakfast," said Kevin.

"You can't do that," I protested, "I've had my smelly feet all over them."

"Oh that's all right, you're in Scotland now," was his reply!

I collected all the cornflakes, remade the bed, and finally got to sleep.

DAY 55 – 28ᵀᴴ AUGUST – GARDENSTOWN TO PETERHEAD

Morning light at Gardenstown – © K Robinson, by kind permission

Up early the next day and, after breakfast (no cornflakes for me) and fond farewells, we walked down to the tiny harbour, got back aboard and were ready to leave for Peterhead by about 9 o'clock.

It sea was flat and a light breeze was blowing as we headed out to sea and along the coast. We were making good progress and were just off Rosehearty when one of the girls shouted, "What's that over there?"

It was a whale!

It was a real Minke whale!

"Ooh, can we go and have a look boss?" asked the girls.

"We can get a bit closer," I said, "but not too close because it's bigger than us and we don't want to get nudged."

A 19 foot boat and a 25 foot whale are not a good combination.

Minke whale ahoy!

Breaching Minke whale
© K Robinson

Kevin had asked us to report any marine life we saw on our way round the coast, and had even given us an identification chart to use as we went round. We recorded the position of the whale, got on the VHF and reported it to Kevin who was chuffed to hear from us, and even more excited to hear about our whale of a find. The area we were sailing through was rich with food for dolphins, whales, basking sharks and other large marine animals, and Kevin's research base monitored the wildlife in the area and also assisted with any rescues and whale or dolphin strandings.

We carried on past Kinnaird Head Lighthouse on the Fraserburgh headland, and then Rattray Head, with its mandatory lighthouse, and huge sand dunes which can be up to 75 feet high and stretch nearly 17 miles from St Combs to Peterhead. This was, in a way, the zenith of our journey. This was where we turned the corner and found ourselves southward bound at last. I must admit I felt my heart leap as I realised I was on my way

"Brookie" the Dolphin frolicking in the Moray Firth
© K Robinson

134

home and I may yet indeed succeed in my adventure. I thought of my conversation with Sir Robin Knox-Johnson and made a mental note to remember to send him a postcard from Peterhead as I had promised several months before.

Peterhead is the eastern most point of Scotland and is a major fishing port and oil industry service support centre. I had found, in my voyage thus far, that harbour masters had great discretion over the payment of harbour fees and, usually, upon hearing my story and what I was trying to achieve, they waived the berthing fee. In my entire trip I only ended up paying for a night's berthing three times, usually in places run, like Peterhead, by local authorities. One would think that businesses would be tougher in this respect and yet the places run with the tax payer's money were those less likely to be charitable. Interesting!

Approaching Fraserburgh

Huge redundant fishing trawlers

Past Fraserburgh and finally heading south

DAY 56 – 29ᵀᴴ AUGUST – PETERHEAD TO STONEHAVEN

From Peterhead we carried on down the coast past Old Slain's Castle on the hilltop just north of Cruden Bay. It is also known as Dracula's Castle as it's believed that Bram Stoker was so inspired by the Castle that it formed the basis for his most famous novel 'Dracula'.

I'd been warned not to stop at Aberdeen as it was focused on the oil industry and was full of large ships. As we passed Aberdeen an oil rig support ship came up behind us and I tried to get out of his way, which I did, but he just kept on changing course, shadowing us and trying to spook us. I was one step away from firing a white flare across his bridge, and I was mightily annoyed, as being so small, and it so large, made us all unsettled and there was absolutely no need to upset my crew just for a few laughs among the crew.

The girls would have like to have stopped at Aberdeen as they had been to University together there and wanted to show me their old digs but, after the incident with the oil support ship, I think we were all glad we hadn't ventured into the harbour, if that was an indication of the reception we might get from the oil industry ship workers.

We had an incident free and steady sail down the coast and reached our destination, Stonehaven, in good light. Stonehaven is one of the most ancient towns in the area and has been the site of many archaeological digs that trace its origins back to prehistoric times with many important fossils found in the area. On that day it looked just like many other busy coastal towns, with quaint whitewashed brick buildings built around the little harbour and with sturdy stone walls, keeping the sea at bay. The girls and I went ashore, me to find fuel and they to find ice cream. I guess one could say we had different priorities at the time!

Once again, the community spirit came to the fore when a man who had watched us come in to the bay, tie up and come ashore offered me a lift to the gas station

Oil support vessel at Aberdeen

Spectacular profile of New Slain's Castle (haunted?)
South of Stonehaven

Hole in the rock

to get the fuel. He refused payment and was simply happy to help. How kind!

We were happy to have a good pub supper and a good night's sleep after what really was, apart from the shadowing oil rig support vessel, an easy day. I hadn't struck any bad weather since the Lochs and was beginning to wonder just when my run of good luck was going to run out.

DAY 57 – 30ᵀᴴ AUGUST – STONEHAVEN TO TAYPORT

We set off, once again, in fairly benign weather on our way to Tayport, just down the river from Dundee, where I was to change my crew. The girls were delighted to sail

Goody box on the go …

with the gennaker flying for the first time and we had a lovely long downwind trip covering nearly 55 miles by the time we made port.

Not far from the entrance to the River Tay, we went round Budden Ness, which is a range danger area with a lot of unexploded ordnance. I had been there before, as Explosive Ordnance Disposal

Georgina, the navigator …

(EOD) had been my area of expertise in the Royal Engineers.

When I had last visited, many years earlier in 1990, I went to Dundee with my Regimental Sergeant Major, WO1 (RSM) Geoff Holroyd RE, and, while there, saw Scott's ship *Discovery*, the ship he had taken to the Antarctic. It was neglected, moored up, covered in tarpaulins and looking grim. As it happened, my RSM was a first rate carpenter and

Gannets in a feeding frenzy at the mouth of the Firth of Tay

joiner and we both thought how nice it would be to have a little piece of wood from such a monumental vessel. We didn't fancy our chances, as we knew that every piece of wood off that ship had history, and even the spare pieces, if there were any, had better uses to be put to, than acting as a souvenir for some history enthusiast. Still, we figured there was no harm in asking, so we had a word with the caretaker.

"No," he said, "I'm absolutely forbidden to let anyone have any."

I put my hand in my pocket, and pulled out a Scottish ten pound note.

I asked him if what I had in my hand would have any influence on his decision, and he paused for a moment and then said, "There's three bits over there, you can have two of them!" Unbeknown to me on return to our barracks, Geoff had furnished two beautiful belaying pins out of these bits of scrap wood and presented one to me on my departure from 33 Engineer Regiment (EOD) – such a lovely touch from my most loyal right hand man – melted my heart at the time …

Now, many years later, I was keen to see what had become of the ship and we came into the river and headed for the marina at Tayport, just inside the river mouth. I didn't want to go all the way up to Dundee so that's where we stopped for the night. That afternoon, we caught the bus into Dundee and visited Scott's ship, which has now been fully restored and was brilliant to visit. *Discovery* was built to survive the ice and was built with cross members below the waterline so that when the ship was squashed by ice, the force was transferred across the ship, keeping the hull intact. One young Royal Navy Petty Officer seconded to Scott's expedition was heard to utter in his typically Southern Irish lilt:

" … Oh I just kept going pretty lively, Sorr, them killers wasn't too healthy company … ", taken from a rare interview with Chief Petty Officer Tom Crean AM RN, concerning his epic solo scamper across the Antarctic ice floes in 1911 to seek help to rescue two friends who were dangerously adrift on a small floe.

Royal Research Ship (RRS) Discovery

And a wonderful piece from T S Eliott's 'The Waste Land':

Who is this third who walks beside you?
When I count, there are only you and I together
But when I look ahead up the white road
There is always another one walking beside you
Gliding wrapt in a brown mantle, hooded
I do not know whether a man or woman -
But who is that on the other side of you?

This referred to the incredible feat when Shackleton, Worsley and Crean, after crossing some 800nm (1300km) of Southern Ocean in a small boat, somehow managed to clamber across the snow-capped mountains of South Georgia, some 40 miles (64km) in 36 hours, to seek help from the Norwegian whaling station at Stromness. Afterwards, Crean simply said, "The Lord brought us home."

At times, albeit in a small way on this challenging voyage, I am learning to know where he was coming from. And yes, at times, I have felt a 'third hand on the tiller' just to ensure that Brookie is pointing *Theo's Future* in the right direction.

DAY 58 - 31ST AUGUST - DUNDEE

The next day it was time for crew change. Georgina's mum and dad, Annabel and Richard arrived and whisked the girls away with waves and farewells.

On the bridge …

Steady as she goes! I prefer this size

Deck lights – constant source of tripping up

Sailor Mess Deck

Captain Robert Falcon Scott,
©By kind permission of Dundee
Heritage Trust, Discovery Point
www.rrsdiscovery.com

Onboard Scientific Laboratory

Scott's cabin

Stoking the boiler

Steam as well as sail!

Scott's ship RRS Discovery at Dundee

Steel knees for extra strength

My next crew turned up in the form of Colonel Tim Weeks OBE, a dear friend who only survives from minute to minute with a wine box under his arm, and two more babes, Anna Woods and Jane Turner. Both of the girls were from my local village Bosham. Jane is a physiotherapist, whom I nicknamed Thumper because she was always on the move and was very keen to do her best. Anna had always wanted to be a pilot in the RAF, and later went off for training,

New pair of babes Anna Woods and Jane Turner on board

which turned out to be short lived, as the government pulled the plug on training programmes as part of the defence cuts.

Tim Weeks is an army friend from way back and, amongst other things, he is responsible for the Midlands Territorial Army Centres. He later introduced Jane to the Territorial Army, where her career has blossomed, and she is currently working with service men and women who have returned injured from operations overseas. Anna has since left the RAF and been snapped up by the Royal Navy!

When he saw the size of the boat Tim couldn't believe that he, who is a very big man, was going to fit in the boat on his own, let alone with me, and two lassies in the forepeak …

Fresh meat!

Fancy boots!

141

CHAPTER 18 – HEADING SOUTH …

Day 59 – 1ˢᵗ September – Tayport to Anstruther

On our first day together, out we went to where, at the entrance to the River Tay, there was a feeding frenzy of fish. There must have been salmon running as we spotted a pod of about thirty dolphins on the hunt. Lots of little fish were being chased by bigger fish and this of course attracted the gannets and other seabirds that had congregated in large flocks, diving below the water and surfacing to gobble their catch. We made our way past this maelstrom of biology and turned south, down the coast past St Andrews, where, according to my map, the farming land along the coast was interspersed with a collection of golf links, no doubt a Mecca for golfing enthusiasts, and possibly a source for the odd stray golf ball, which hopefully wouldn't make it out to sea as far as our little boat.

Being the first day with new crew on board, I hadn't planned a long jaunt and we had a relaxing sail down round the coast to Anstruther for the night, which had a well protected marina tucked in off the exposed coast. I realised at this point that I didn't have the charts for Edinburgh, where we were due to visit a school for the blind. Fortunately our neighbour in the marina that night, a local yachtsman called Rob had a full set of charts and allowed me to borrow them for the voyage. How generous he was, and we swapped addresses so I could post them back when I had finished with them.

Tim Weeks (alias 'swift and bold') looking for action …

Two babes and Tim …

DAY 60 – 2ND SEPTEMBER – ANSTRUTHER TO EYEMOUTH

Anstruther is only just up the coast from our next destination Edinburgh. I had planned this as we wanted to spend a large part of the day visiting a school for blind children when we got there. On our way across the Firth of Forth towards Edinburgh I made a phone call to confirm the details for our visit to the school, only to be told, very apologetically, by the lady on the other end of the phone, that the school was in fact for deaf and not blind children.

"Oh," I said, rather taken aback, "I see."

And so, apparently, could the children.

Well, when I shared this revelation with the crew, they fell about laughing. I thought about whether we should carry on into Edinburgh, which really was further inland than we needed to go, and decided to change course and continue south across the firth, past yet more golfing establishments at North Berwick and on down the coast.

With calm seas and a brisk sou'westerly, Anna and Jane finally had time to get the hang of Mike's sea shanty, 'Farewell Spanish Ladies', while Tim came closer to jumping overboard because of it!

Once again we had an opportunity to fly Sir Turtle and the girls were delighted to hoist the gennaker as we sailed downwind. On the way round St Abb's Head, however, we made a mess of a jibe which snapped the gennaker pole, a wooden pole used to hold the sail out away from the boat. Sir Turtle was forced to retire for the day but, luckily, we weren't far from our port for that night and we motored into Eyemouth, which is on the border between Scotland and England.

Eyemouth is a lovely friendly fishing port and Chal Chute, true to form, had rung ahead and spoken to the harbour master, who came out to meet us in his launch, took us

Gennaker pole emergency repairs in Eyemouth

alongside and gave us a very heartening welcome. The little village was delightful and there were even fat seals swimming in the harbour scrounging for fish scraps off the many fishing boats that were berthed there.

Once we were safely tied up we had a go at fixing the snapped gennaker pole by binding it in a kind of splint, which didn't unfortunately work that well. We did the best with what we had but I wasn't happy with the repair and it would have to wait to be mended properly at a later date.

DAY 61 – 3ʳᵈ SEPTEMBER – EYEMOUTH TO HOLY ISLAND

Those boots were made for ...

Next morning, we sailed down past Berwick-upon-Tweed, the northernmost town of England and, as such, the site of many a hostile takeover. Further down the coast and out to sea a little way, we could see the Farne Islands but, just north of these, just off the mainland, separated by treacherous sandbanks and shallow water, is Holy Island, with Lindisfarne Castle and Lindisfarne Priory. It is well worth a visit so we sailed round Emmanuel Head, very carefully I might add, as there is a maze of craggy rocks that protrude down past the castle up on the hill and out into the bay where we tentatively set the anchor. I say tentatively because, before I beach the boat, I always do a reconnaissance, as the last thing you want to do is find

Pitch black night but still smiling ...

Dawn over Lindisfarne Castle

144

Shore party ... Wet bum on the cards!

*Great castle visit ... spot the teddy
bear in each room!*

your boat has settled on the top of some old anchor or rock, potentially putting a hole in the boat. Fortunately we had arrived in time to watch the tide fall away from the beach, and while we then had to wait overnight for the tide to return, it meant we were also able to pick the best spot on the beach to set the boat with fore and aft anchors the next day.

Day 62 – 4ᵗʰ September – Holy Island

"Tonight," I said the next morning, "we're going up on the beach and we'll have the best night's sleep you can ever imagine, because there'll be no water around us!"

We waited for the tide, picked a spot, put the kedge over the back, went forward on it till it held, put the main anchor over the bow and went

Holy Island hulks converted into fishermen's stores

A shared moment at the Abbey

PRAYER for PEACE

LEAD me from Death to Life,
from Falsehood to Truth
+
Lead me from Despair to Hope,
from Fear to Trust.
+
Lead me from Hate to Love,
from War to Peace.
+
Let Peace fill our Heart,
our World, our Universe...
+
PEACE, PEACE, PEACE.

back till the boat was well secured. We waited for her to settle and clambered down on the mud to walk ashore, dragging our dinghy behind us. We were back in England!

We spent the day walking the hills, visiting the Castle (with hidden teddy bears in each room to find), some rather interesting and quite famous upturned old wooden fishing boat hulks, converted into fishermen's stores and generally having a good explore of the island. Jane Turner had lost her mother to cancer not long before the trip and I was still missing Simon terribly, so the two of us went into the priory at one point, and said a little prayer and lit a candle. Grief is terrible, but can be made less so with the company of a good friend who is able to understand how you feel.

On the landward side of Holy Island is a causeway so that the tourists can make their way over to the island when the tide is favourable. In the middle of the causeway the locals have built a scaffold tower, with a telephone at the top, so that if you find yourself halfway along the causeway and the tide comes in, which it does very quickly because it is so flat, you can climb the tower and call for help and someone will come out to get you in a boat! You pay for this unique rescue service in the pub afterwards …

You may remember that, in Port St Mary on the Isle of Man, weeks earlier, I had met Simon Tuck, another ex serviceman, who had done a marvellous job of fundraising for me, when I was exhausted. He had sent me and my crew off for a curry dinner while he did all the hard work and, as we departed his company, he dared me to do a 'moonie,' drop my pants for money, saying that if he saw a photo of my buttocks on the website he would donate another 40 quid to the cause. So there on Holy Island, I was finally persuaded, against my better judgment, to drop my pants and put a picture of my derriere on the website. The girls promised not to look and Tim used a felt tip pen to draw a face and so, in the best possible taste, and in the most discrete way possible, I posed for my photo. (Not sure now that Holy Island was the most appropriate place for such activity but I was careful to keep my backside pointed away from the priory!).

The net effect of this frivolity was that I earned another £40 but, in the process, lost $1,000 as the American paint company that had sponsored me for $1,000 later saw the offending image and withdrew their sponsorship funds, saying they couldn't possibly be involved with a charity that allowed such lewd behaviour.

This was very upsetting, really, as the supposed lewd image is really no worse than the average plumber's crack seen everywhere in the world. I would have thought that such a silly exercise, done simply to raise more money for the charity, could not really be labelled offensive, so I'd love to hear from them if they read this and reconsider their actions.

Anyway, unaware of what was to come as a consequence of our day, we had a good feed in the local pub, and made our way back to the boat

The "Moon's a balloon" … but an extra £40 in the kitty from Simon Tuck, Port St Mary, Isle of Man

where we had a jolly evening, watching a James Bond movie on my laptop as the tide went out once more and left us high and dry on the beach for the night.

My claim that the crew would have the best sleep of their lives proved to be somewhat untrue as the boat came to rest heeling to one side. Anna and Tim were left uncomfortable and rather low in the boat while Jane and I enjoyed the good view over their heads. This made sleeping arrangements rather interesting, with Tim creating a blockade to keep him in bed and the girls lying width ways across the fore peak V-shaped bunk. I, however, was left in a comfortable and safe position and had an uninterrupted night's sleep!

Not really built to fit in here ...

Day 63 – 5ᵗʰ September – Holy Island to Tynemouth

Upon leaving Holy Island on the outgoing tide very early the next morning, we made an attempt at sailing out to the Farne Islands, as there's a little chapel on the main island of St Cuthbert's that we thought we

Anna pinched my hat ...

might visit. The Farne Islands are famous for their puffins and other marine wildlife, as well as for the story of Grace Darling. The story goes that Grace Darling, the daughter of a lighthouse keeper, was in Longshore Lighthouse on Longstone Rock, one of the outer Farne Islands, when she spotted the wreck and survivors of the *Forfarshire* on Big Harcar, a nearby low rocky island. The *Forfarshire*, a steamship, had foundered on the rocks in the gale and broken in half, with one half having already sunk. The nearest lifeboat was at Seashouses, and it was too rough for the lifeboat to reach the islands where the boat had foundered. She and her father set off in a rowing boat and rescued nine survivors off the rocks. Even though she was not a member of the lifeboat service, she was awarded a Silver Medal by that amazing organisation in recognition of her exceptional bravery.

I can tell you from experience that the currents that weave around the islands are very strong and, whilst we were there, the weather was favourable; I would hate to think what it would be like in a storm, especially around the outer islands. As it was, I thought there was a chance we could get the boat through and round the currents to the beach but I was almost certain our little boat, with its small engine wouldn't be able to get out again. So, much to the disappointment of my crew, we headed away, back on a southerly course, leaving our visit for another day. It really was a case of safety first, sightseeing second.

On down the coast we sailed, watching the cliffs and beaches fall away behind us on our starboard side. With our early start and good sailing conditions, we were making great progress and I decided to head for Tynemouth, a good 60 miles from where we had set off that morning. I knew that I could get into Tynemouth in the dark as it has a well lit entrance with walls built to define the mouth of the river and keep the ocean swell at bay. So, wishing to make the most of the favourable wind and sea state, we kept going.

Tynemouth is literally that, found at the mouth of the River Tyne. This area is well utilised with large numbers of vessels travelling up and down the river to Newcastle, or Newcastle upon Tyne as it is formally called. The Royal Quays Marina, where we stayed, was not right at the river's mouth but, rather, up the river and round the bend a little way, closer to Newcastle.

My crew were departing the next day so we went ashore and had a last pleasant evening together. I was delighted when Anna and Jane presented me with another mascot for the journey. *Theo's Future* now had a ginger ship's cat to keep the rats at bay and it was promptly named Mrs Chippy, after the cat that accompanied Shackleton's crew on their voyage to Antarctica. Mrs Chippy joined Daisy's dolphin and the many other soft toys and mascots I had acquired on the journey so far. Soon I was going to run out of room for real crew!

DAY 64 – 6TH SEPTEMBER TYNEMOUTH

The next day Major Richard Peters, a dear old army friend, former trans-ocean crewmate and Georgina's father, joined me in the pouring rain. We had many sea miles under our belts when he had sailed with me across the Atlantic in *Never Look Back*. Richard is a great story teller, though sometimes a little too long winded in his efforts, and there have been times when I've had to say, "Come on Richard, give us the punch line, we want to get to the pub!"

He had wanted to sail the north east of England with me, an area where he had family connections, and also where he had served with the Light Infantry in the Territorial Army.

Upon his arrival, we stowed his gear and went ashore for a fish 'n chip supper in an old ferry that was moored in the marina as a floating restaurant.

Back in Port Patrick I had met a lady who told me of her daughter, who ran a recreation centre near Newcastle for blind people. "If you give her a ring, I'm sure she'd love to meet you and show you around the centre," she'd said, so I gave her daughter a ring and we organised to visit the centre the next day.

Storm clouds brewing for the nth time ... Please not again

CHAPTER 19 – THE WIDOW'S MITE …

Day 65 – 7ᵀᴴ September Tynemouth

Richard and I caught a train to Sunderland, where we were met by Lesley, of Actionaires, and she drove us off to her centre. One of the first people I bumped into was a Royal Marine Colour Sergeant who had lost his sight in the Korean War. Both being Royal Marines meant we had plenty to talk about … HooArrr.

I gave a little talk about what I was doing and had a wonderfully enthusiastic reception. There was plenty of banter and story-telling, and I found it quite humbling to be there with a group of blind people when I was sailing around the UK to raise money for my blind godson and others like him.

When we went to leave, many of the people wanted to make a donation. Just as we were about to go, I felt a tug at my sleeve and a little old lady had found me in the crowd and said quietly, "Mike, I'm so impressed with what you're doing. I don't have much but I'd like to make a small donation and share my housekeeping money with you." She had in her hand a five pound note and said, "If I give you this £5 note, can you give me three pounds in change?"

Richard and I were quite taken aback and rummaged around for some change for her. It brought a tear to my eye that this elderly lady, who didn't have much, wanted to share what she had. Truly, here was a shining example of 'the widow's mite' in real life.

Having been humbled, fed, and educated from a morning of bumping into blind people and hearing their inspiring stories of battling through life, and, in some cases, them bumping into us, we retraced our steps and made our way back to the boat.

Newcastle's famous landmark

"Wow!" I thought on my way back on the train, "Life has a meaning." Strange to think that a chance meeting with an elderly lady on a coach trip in a Port Patrick pub

Presenting two belaying pins for blind members to touch and feel our exceptional maritime heritage

Handing over some "Whacky Practicals" tactile items for blind members to enjoy

would see me travelling to visit a centre for the blind on the other side of the country and experience such generosity as the old lady who shared her housekeeping with us. Amazing!

By the time we made it back to the marina, it was getting late and we'd had enough of walking and catching buses, so we ate again in the ferry restaurant at the marina before heading back to the boat for a good night's sleep.

DAY 66 – 8TH SEPTEMBER TYNEMOUTH TO HARTLEPOOL

We left the mouth of the Tyne and I remember it was a murky day as we made our way down the coast past Sunderland through grey drizzle. We spent most of the day in light winds motor sailing on what was really just a horrible, wet, dirty and depressing day. It was quite a let-down after the buzz of the day before and we struggled to make any progress.

We kept going and we kept going. We had no choice really.

The light was fading and the tide was turning, and in the distance I could just see St Hilda's church high on the limestone cliffs on the headland above Hartlepool.

"Come on St Hilda," I said to myself, "Give us a hand. Get us in here 'cos we've had enough."

We were wet, we were tired and we'd just spent the last hour trying to negotiate the tides and find the entrance to the lock, with the lights of the town behind the marina confusing us. Richard eventually spotted the green starboard channel marker and we were able to make our way in, only to find the marina was shut and we had to ring to get the lock gates opened. Fortunately Chal had, once again, done his stuff and the marina manager knew we were coming and he came to open the lock.

We sat in the boat as the water of the lock rose. We were drenched, hungry, tired and had simply had enough.

It was just one of those "had enough" days.

From start to finish I'd had enough!

By eleven o'clock that night, when we finally made it in to our berth at the Hartlepool Marina, I had definitely had enough!

After sorting out our berthing with the marina manager we came out of the office and I saw a big brass monkey sitting on a post a few feet out in the water. The monkey was holding a bowl and I asked the marina manager what the statue was doing there.

"Ooharrr, now there's a story," said the marina manager, as he proceeded to tell me the story.

Way back in the French wars, somewhere round the mid 1700s, a French ship foundered off St Hilda's Point, with all hands lost. The only survivor was the ship's monkey, which was found on the beach wearing a red jacket. "Red jacket," thought the locals, "that's what British infantry soldiers wear. He must be a spy!"

So the monkey was caught and put in prison. The townspeople decided that the monkey should be tried for espionage. So, the monkey was put on trial! The jury found him guilty and the judge sentenced the monkey to be hung at dawn. So, of course, the monkey was taken out the next morning and hung. Now, even to this day, if you come from Hartlepool you are nicknamed a 'monkey hanger'!

By the marina, the town had built a big bronze monkey holding a bowl and placed it on a post in the water just out of reach from the marina steps. If you can toss a coin into the bowl, it's considered good luck. "Mind you," said the Marina Manager at the end of his story, "We have to clean it out regularly or the local drunks use a kiddie's fishing net to scoop the coins out and buy their booze!"

I felt better after that little story and, fortunately, we saw a little pub that was still open and we went straight there and had ourselves a pint. Probably one of the most enjoyed drinks in the entire trip. Washed down with some sausages and chips we went back to the boat in a far better frame of mind than when we had disembarked.

DAY 67 – 9ᵀᴴ SEPTEMBER HARTLEPOOL TO WHITBY

In the morning, we couldn't leave Hartlepool without a visit to *HMS Trincomalee*, Britain's oldest warship and the only remaining Nelsonian frigate, which was, at the time, kept in a dry dock and in the process of being restored. Round the edge of the dock there was a fabulous display depicting all the activities involved in getting a ship ready for sea – highly recommended if you're ever in the neighbourhood.

A first glimpse of HMS Trincomalee

Despite the fact we delayed our departure by a couple of hours, it was well worth it. We went back to pay our dues at the marina office but the manager generously waved his hand and said,

Richard with one of the 8 heavy 32 pounder solid shot guns on HMS Trincomalee

The last surviving Nelsonian frigate

154

On board with the Chief Bosun's Mate carrying out necessary maintenance

Hartlepool's monkey ... thank you for your donations

"I'm not going to charge you for your stay here. I've had a word with the local council and they've decided you can have the takings from the monkey's bowl for the last three months, and here it is!"

bowl for the last three months, and here it is!"

He handed over a sack full of copper coins, which weighed as much as another person, or two! I had use a rope to lower it down to Richard on the boat and I'm sure the boat was lower in the water once it was stowed.

The thing about a bag of coins is that it takes a long time to count and it took us a couple of days to do so and when I finally did haul it to a bank, they were not that happy to see it!

Fab support once more from the coxswain of the Whitby Lifeboat

The wind was building and, because we had taken the time to visit the ship, we were running late. I'd broken one of my key rules and missed the turn of the tide so, as a result, we had a long way to go with the conditions not in our favour.

As luck would have it, the wind was on the nose and it was blowing and building. We had thirty miles to go in a 19 foot boat with half the day gone and the wind from the wrong direction. I knew it was going to be a long day.

We spent hour after hour tacking in, tacking out, tacking in, tacking out. None of this relaxing downwind sailing where you watch the shore slip by as the wind pushes us from behind. So once again it was dark and we were exhausted by the

Towards the end of yet another long day at sea ...

Richard – loyal crew member

Whitby Historic Civic Building

time we made it to our destination. We rounded up at the entrance to Whitby Harbour at 11 o'clock that night, and dropped the sails. We motored in through the moles and cheekily picked up a mooring for the night, hoping we wouldn't offend anyone if we were caught in the morning. "Right," said Richard, "I'm knackered and so are you. We're not going ashore tonight, I'm going to make a pasta." Richard, fortunately, is a very good cook so he whipped up a tuna pasta. I dug out a bottle of wine from my supplies and we feasted together before falling into a deep, and no doubt tuneful sleep, though I can't remember hearing Richard snore because we both slept solidly till morning.

DAY 68 – 10ᵀᴴ SEPTEMBER WHITBY TO SCARBOROUGH

I woke up quite early next morning and I felt quite strange because everything seemed to make sense and I felt quite comfortable in my surroundings. Perhaps I was finally feeling at home in the fuggy, dishevelled interior of my boat! God knows we had been through enough together and shared plenty of time in close confines.

Whatever the reason, I woke feeling that this was going to be a good day.

Whitby is the home of Captain James Cook and I have always greatly admired him as a sailor, an explorer, a navigator and a master mariner. By the age of 21, he was already commissioned as a ship's officer, almost unheard of in his day. King George III, aware that parts of the world were

Captain Cook Museum

Scaled down replica of HMS Endeavour

being discovered and claimed for other nations, decided he should be in on the act and commissioned Lieutenant James Cook RN to take a converted coal ship, the *Endeavour*, on a voyage of discovery and, in some ways, he is responsible for the wide expanse of today's Commonwealth. One of his famous ditties goes like this:

"I Keep Six Honest Serving Men"
I keep six honest serving men (they taught me all I know);
Their names are What and Why and When
And How and Where and Who.
I send them over land and sea,
I send them east and west;
But after they have worked for me,
I give them all a rest.

Captain James R Cook RN
1728 - 1779

Richard and I spent a few hours that morning in the Captain Cook Museum, which was fantastic as I have always found him to be such an inspirational figure. Throughout life, we all need heroes and this man is one of my all time heroes. He was once heard to say:

" ... I had the ambition not only to go farther than anyone had been before, but as far as it was possible to go ... " and " ... You are never giving, nor can you give, enough service ... "

Captain Cook was probably the greatest ever British pioneering navigator and explorer who commanded three major voyages of discovery, charting and naming many islands in the Pacific Ocean, including New Zealand and parts of Australia, as well as claiming them for the crown. He also sailed along the coast of North America as far as the Bering Strait. Interestingly, he is also credited with remedies for the prevention of scurvy at sea.

Yes, not surprisingly, we were once again late to leave for the second day in a row. So much for my tidal gate rule!

It was lunchtime by the time we left, heading for Scarborough, which luckily, was not too far down the coast. The wind

Scarborough's delightful "Dive Belle" statue

once again was not cooperating but was not as bad as the day before. Today, at least, we were able to sail and make our way south rather than having to beat our way down the coast. Thank God for that, as we had tacked enough the day before to last us a week or more. We rounded the big headland with the castle at the top that protected the town from the sea and headed into the little harbour of Scarborough.

On the far side of the harbour was a replica pirate ship, which was used for trips around the bay. Being widely built with a kind of bustle at the back it seemed an ideal vessel to raft up to so we moored alongside feeling relatively secure.

We went ashore and I had a wander around before linking up with the Scarborough Sailing Club where we spent a very

Pirate ship: The Hispaniola. Richard with Captain Morgan, a notorious one handed pirate

pleasant evening and shared a story or two over some drinks.

Scarborough is one of the real seaside towns, with Punch and Judy shows, donkey rides, colourful merry-go-rounds and sideshow attractions. People have been going there for their summer holidays for years and you can just imagine the striped bathing huts being wheeled down to the water's edge for the ladies to modestly dip their toe in the water without being seen.

I woke with a start in the middle of the night and got a huge fright when the sound of gushing water reached my ears through the darkness. With my heart beating wildly in my chest I leapt out of bed and peered outside to see the boat next door having a pee into our cockpit! The pirate ship we had tied up to had an automatic bilge pump, with the outlet, unbeknownst to us, positioned directly above the cockpit of our boat. I was woken by the sound of water pouring into the cockpit and splashing down the companionway.

I quickly shut the hatch to stop the water coming inside and clambered back into bed. Fortunately the cockpit is almost impossible to flood as the outboard engine well allows excess water to drain away quickly. Whatever next!

DAY 69 – 11TH SEPTEMBER - SCARBOROUGH TO BRIDLINGTON

The next morning we were back on task and paying attention again. I had to get the tide right because today we had to go round Flamborough Head, which is a bit of a carbuncle that sticks out from the coast. What does a carbuncle do? Well, they're not really wanted on a human form, but when they form a bump on a coastline they cause tidal constriction, and that means that off the end of Flamborough Head you get a rip or a race. I had been warned, "Brookie, watch out for the water off Flamborough Head. You can get a nasty sea there."

Thankfully, the day was not particularly rough and we went down and clawed our way out towards the head and I wondered what on earth we were going to find. I'd never been there, never seen it and all the nasty stories made you nervous. We kept looking for white water as we could feel the swell and the power of the sea underneath us but there weren't any breaking waves and we were able to make our way through the most dangerous area without mishap. We were extremely lucky and it was almost a Neptune's deputy moment and someone was looking out for us! It's definitely one of those tricky ones, a Portland Bill, a Land's End. Off Flamborough Head is a serious piece of water.

Amazingly, it was about 4 o'clock in the afternoon when we rounded Flamborough Head and made our way in to the tiny entrance that guards the ancient port of Bridlington, tucked in around the other side. We found a place to moor, and were in safe and sound, quite pleased with ourselves. We had made it around Flamborough Head in one piece.

We went ashore and gorged ourselves on fresh seafood. Being a fishing town there was a lot to choose from, freshly caught that day. We slept well and we felt like we were finally getting the miles under our belt. I felt that Flamborough Head was a significant milestone, another major step in my homeward journey, and the realisation that I was nearing home began to form in my mind.

The Pilot's Prayer

The Lord is my pilot, I shall not drift
He lighteth me across the dark waters;
He steereth me in the deep channels, He keepeth my log,
He guideth me by the star of holiness for his namesake.
Yea though I sail though the thunders and tempests of life,
I shall dread no danger, for thou art with me,
Thy love and Thy care, they shelter me.
Thou preparest a harbour for me in the homeland of eternity.
Thou anointest the waves with oil, my ship runneth calmly .
Surely sunlight and starlight shall favour me in the voyage I take,
And I shall rest in the port of my God forever.
Amen

CHAPTER 20 – HOMEWARD BOUND …

DAY 70 – 12TH SEPTEMBER - BRIDLINGTON TO GRIMSBY

After a good breakfast of Brookie's porridge, we set off out of Bridlington straight across the bay, round Spurn Head, which is low lying and hard to see from a distance. The peninsula is made up from eroded sand and shingle washed down the coastline from Flamborough Head. It curves in from the coastline and extends nearly three and a half miles across the mouth of the Humber Estuary. Many an unwary vessel has come to grief in poor weather, and there is a lifeboat station tucked in at Spurn Head to cater for the number of casualties. The most decorated RNLI crewman in the country is based there, which says a lot for its popularity as a shipwreck destination.

The weather this day, however, was manageable and we gave Spurn Head a wide berth to ensure we didn't run into trouble. We had another good day's sail to Grimsby, which is on the south bank of the Humber River and was once one of England's main fishing ports.

We pulled in to the old fishing harbour and as, we sailed in, saw an amazing old brick building. Standing huge, derelict, and oddly positioned on the sea wall, almost straddling the edge of the water, I had no idea what role it could have played in the past and was determined to find out more about it. We were welcomed to Grimsby by members of the local sailing club and I asked one of the chaps what the building was for. "Oh," he said, "that was the largest ice factory ever built." He went on to explain that the fishing trawlers would line up, ten at a time, and collect their ice before they left for the fishing grounds.

Soirée time on board Theo's Future

It's all closed down now but one can imagine what it would have looked like with ten trawlers filling their holds with ice from the chutes on the side of the building, while ten more lined up behind waiting for their turn.

Grimsby was another crew change stopover and it was time for Richard to depart. As a self-employed gardener, he's never one to beat around the bush, so when we got to Grimsby he packed up his bits and said, "Right Brookie, I have to go," and off he went. No messing around, he simply had things to do. Richard could always be relied on to give you his utmost efforts while a project was on, but switched almost immediately to his next task when the job was done. He's always been like that and has to be one of the most focused people I know. I only found out after the trip that he had in fact forgotten to bring a sleeping bag with him and yet he hadn't once complained. When I look back at the atrocious wet conditions he had to put up with, I am most impressed. I think he would admit though that he would prefer to include a sleeping bag in his kit should there be a next time …

With Richard's swift departure I had a rare night by myself and, as I do enjoy my own company from time to time, it was quite pleasant to not have to worry about anyone but me.

DAY 71 - 13ᵀᴴ SEPTEMBER – GRIMSBY

I also had most of the next day off, while I waited for my new crew to arrive, so was able to spread out a few things to air and tidy parts of the boat.

Joining me later were my two new crewmembers, David Moore and Jilly Rumble - "Rumble in the Jungle". Hard to believe, but Jilly Rumble had come back for more punishment! I obviously hadn't beaten her enough with the cat-o'-nine-tails on the first leg she did with me because she wanted more! She said when she arrived, "I crewed for you in the west country, so I'm going to crew for you in the east!"

David Moore, my other sailing companion, and I have been friends for years and had sailed many miles together, helping each other out in the past when we needed to deliver a boat to various places including the Canaries. He is a musician and had retired as a Colour Sergeant and Band Master from the Royal Marines after a full 22-year career in the army, playing the

David Moore – fellow Royal Marine and Mariner

David studying where to go (or not to go!)

Rumble in the jungle …
(Jilly's sleeping quarters)

clarinet and the saxophone in the Royal Marines band. After his stint in the RM, he worked as the music teacher at Lancing College, which is where Oscar Nowak went, hence the connection that saw Oscar sailing with me. David has always affectionately been known as Tubby Moore as he has no height but plenty of width and is incredibly strong. In the forces, everyone gets a nickname and he was also known as Pony Moore, because the Moors are famous for their ponies … obviously!

As David stepped aboard *Theo's Future*, one problem became immediately obvious. He's short and stout and the entrance to the cabin with spray hood up is very restrictive. "What you do David is go in head first, put your hands on the centreboard case and crawl in on your hands and knees," I told him.

"OK", he said with a very unconvinced tone in his voice, "I'll give it a go."

In the end, David came up with his own solution. He put his hands on the cockpit seats and his feet up on the centreboard and just walked out on all fours. It seemed to work in reverse order for getting in, which solved the cabin problem.

Jilly had plenty of experience already from her previous voyage

One of the last remaining Grimsby trawlers

and rebuilt her hamster's nest in the forepeak with her own private entrance through the fore hatch.

"Right," I said when the two of them had stowed their gear and familiarised themselves with the boat, "We've got the rest of the day, so let's go and look at this great fishing town."

We wandered into town and went to the museum, where we saw a full sized Grimsby Trawler on the river outside and a great exhibition of all the activities related to fishing, which is, I think, a seriously evil, grotty but necessary business. Inside the museum, there is one exhibit I will never forget. You go through a door and suddenly you're on the heaving deck of a trawler, you can hardly stand up, it's freezing cold and it smells, and you can't wait to get out. Just one short experience was more than enough to put me off and I was glad I hadn't been born into a fishing family. Having said that, we had an amazing fish supper that evening at Leon's Fish Restaurant. Delicious!

Sad news arrived that evening when I heard of the death of Nick Sherman's daughter Alexandra, who had been born with a number of disabilities and been courageously nursed through to the age

Arctic conditions – David holding on tight

Chef! Trawler delights for crew's evening scram

Love at first sight! ... Naughty Jilly

Storing fish at sea ... a very smelly business

of 31 by Nick and his wife, Rosie. I knew they would be desperately sad and Alexandra was their only child.

I was torn as to whether I should go back to support Nick and Rosie in their grief and I talked about what I should do with David and Jilly. They were happy to let me go and said they would wait for me at Grimsby or David suggested he could sail on down the coast and I could rejoin them later.

I realised then that I didn't want them to do that; I needed to get on with my voyage, and I realised I had to complete every leg for myself or I would feel cheated of the chance to say that I had truly sailed around the country, instead adding oh … except for the bit along the Norfolk coast.

I rang Nick and we talked for a while and he agreed that I should stay and carry on with my mission. He knew that he and Rosie would be in my thoughts and prayers and, while he valued my offer to come, there was little I could actually do. Such is the way with death, especially of a loved one, as there really is nothing anyone can do, but go on living.

It was while we were in Grimsby that I saw a stark but fitting reminder of death's place in the lives of the locals. The Grimsby Fisherman's Memorial is a fantastic sculpture by Trevor Harries that depicts the side of a fishing boat with nets filled with fish hanging down into the sea, and a grim faced fisherman in full sou'wester hauling the load up over the side of the boat. The carved inscription says it all:

I cannot bend beside the grave;
For he sleeps in a secret sea.
And not one gentle whispering wave,
Will tell the place to me.

But though unseen by human eyes,
And mortals know it not,
His Father knoweth where he lies,
And angels guard the spot.

Dedicated 16th January 2005

The whole town's life revolved around the fishing industry and generation after generation of men had gone to sea and, in some cases, never come home. Life in the town never stopped, however, because of the tragedies that occurred. Fish still needed to be caught, nets still needed mending, and the living got on with doing just that.

Beside Grimsby's Fisherman's Memorial with David Moore and Jilly Rumble (2nd stint, coming back for more)

So with mixed emotions I went to sleep that night, thinking of Nick and Rosie, remembering my own dear son, who I missed terribly, and thinking of the hundreds of others that had died, leaving behind sadness and grief. Perhaps, in some small way, I was able to put life more into perspective, accepting the inevitability of death, and the need to go on living as best one can, while one still can …

Day 72 – 14ᵀᴴ September - Grimsby to Wells-next-the-Sea

We left the next morning heading south, intent on passing The Wash, a well known piece of rough water off the Norfolk coast, caused by water being swept in and out of a large bay with three roughly straight sides meeting at right angles, each about 15 miles (25 km) in length. The bay is not very deep as a result of the silt washed down from several rivers and, with many changing sandbanks, the sea off the mouth of this large bay is often wild and unpredictable. The aim of the day was to safely negotiate this rather dangerous stretch of water and make our way to a little town called Wells-next-the-Sea.

The problem with The Wash is the tide from the south washes in and sweeps round the corner, and the sea from the north behaves in a similar fashion. The water here, being shallow, tends to stand up and form quite large waves, which, when colliding with the waves reflected off the side walls of the bay from other directions creates a maelstrom of water that is ricocheted out towards the open sea, making life in a boat very uncomfortable indeed.

To complicate matters further, the shallow water has been used to build huge wind farms, made up of hundreds of turbines lined up as far as the eye can see. It is forbidden to sail through a wind farm area and yet this often means sailing around them, through dangerous areas that one would otherwise avoid. Such is the case with The Wash, and I suppose one could say we knew we had been through the wash by the time we got to the other side because it definitely felt like we had spent several hours in a washing machine!

Jilly, bless her cotton socks, had no breakfast that morning, claiming she was still full from dinner the night before.

"You must eat something," I said, "even if it's only a bit of bread."

"No," she said, "I'll be fine."

Well … she wasn't.

In fact, far from it.

The gap across The Wash is a good twenty miles from Skegness south towards our destination. Poor Jilly … she spewed, and she spewed, and she spewed.

I felt so sorry for her but we couldn't stop, we couldn't change anything, we were motor-sailing as best we could and she just had to put up with it. I always find it better for people to sit out in the fresh air if they are feeling seasick as claustrophobia in enclosed spaces, stale air and the inability to see the horizon all contribute to making one feel even more sick. Jilly however refused to come out of the boat and sit in the cockpit, so had to make do with a bucket for company downstairs in the boat. Not a pleasant ride at all!

It was 8 o'clock and the light was fading by the time we arrived off the coast from the river that led to our destination for the night. I had been warned not to attempt to go into the estuary once the ebb had started as the area was known for its treacherous sandbanks and strong currents but we were knackered and Jilly was very unwell, and I was quite worried about her as she was getting dehydrated from throwing up so much and not being able to keep anything down. Luckily, David has always had a cast iron stomach and I was able to run the boat around him while he steered, but we had to put into somewhere for the night and we were running out of options.

We paused at the entrance to the river estuary and David and I discussed the situation. There was quite a bit of ambient light from the moon and stars, and our eyes had adjusted so we could see quite well. We decided to give it a go so we motored into the estuary with the 5 hp engine going full bore.

The depth sounder stopped working because of the current rushing past the transducer under the boat. We were part way up the river when we realized the GPS wasn't working either as it had us sitting on dry land. We were only just making headway. David and I looked at each other and realised it was time to dig deep. It was dark, the current was against us, we had a sick crew member and we were all in need of some dry land and, better still, some dry land with a pub because, by then, I could have murdered a pint. "We can do this," we told each other.

Between us, David and I managed to negotiate the bends in the river and fought our way up against the tide. Fortunately, the boat needed very little water to float so, while there were sandbanks to be avoided, we didn't have a deep keel that could get caught, so there was little chance of getting pinned for the night. David was up by the mast acting as look out in the dark, talking me along so we didn't crash into anything. Suddenly he shouted, "Mike, helm over! Quick!" So, instinctively, I threw the tiller over to port, and then saw this huge mud bank right in front of us, with the bow sprit just managing to scrape its way past as we turned. We had been a nanosecond from spearing the mud bank with the bowsprit. We would have been stuck like a toothpick or worse still snapped the bowsprit. My heart just about stopped.

"Wow Brookie, that was close!" called David.

"Well, you're supposed to be on lookout!"

"Don't blame me, I couldn't see a bloody thing!"

As we came round the bend, suddenly there in front of us was the town. We were just wondering where to moor when Dave spotted three flashes from a torch … a traditional smugglers' signal that we reciprocated … could it be for us? We had no barrels of brandy to roll up the beach but we continued cautiously until someone called out, "Hello Mike." What a relief that it wasn't a trap by the 'boys in blue!'

We were very pleased to have made it and pleased also to see Roy and Sheila Sherlock, who were standing on the dock with flashlights in hand waiting to greet us. It was late but they had already organised a table at one of the local restaurants that was staying open late especially to accommodate us. David and I had a fabulous meal after a hard day at sea but poor Jilly didn't feel much like food. I felt bad as a skipper because I don't like any of my crew to get sea sick but one can only give advice and offer food and pills that will assist them; and at the end of the day, we all learn from experience. Luckily, it doesn't seem to have put her off sailing, though I must admit she was extremely happy to see her husband, when he arrived to pick her up the next day and, perhaps at the time, the thought of home, on land, in a house, was more endearing than the thought of getting back on the boat and putting to sea.

Jilly had organised to accompany me for just a short jaunt (or rather haunt) on this occasion, so she didn't leave because of her bad experience. Fortunately, Jilly departing in the morning meant David and I had a day in Wells-next the-Sea to rest, explore, and wait for our next companion. I even had time to go to the shops and splashed out on a new pair of sea boots and some lovely Norwegian woolly socks. We needed the day to get ourselves together for, though it may not have sounded particularly dramatic, the complication of Jilly being sick certainly made the trip far more stressful. It had to be one of the most unpleasant experiences of my whole trip. I also took the opportunity to do some work on the electrical system and bought some bits and pieces to improve the setup of the batteries on the boat.

Later that day we met up with the harbour master and when we introduced ourselves he said, "Oh … so you're Mike Brooke. Mr Chute contacted us and said you were coming, but … you shouldn't be here. Did you come up this river last night? That's against the local bylaw. I really ought to be giving you a ticket … but you're here … well done, but very foolhardy."

He had to be seen to give us a bollicking but, with a twinkle in his eye, he added, "Here's the key, free showers, help yourself."

So off we went and had a hot shower, and washed our clothes but I couldn't help reflecting on what he had said.

As is often the case there really was no alternative to coming up the river and none was suggested. In some cases these bylaws are really nonsensical because, if I had had somewhere else to go, I would have gone there and the idea that anyone in their right mind would attempt to hove-to for the night in The Wash is beyond comprehension. This, complicated by Jilly's illness, reassured me that we really had done the only thing we could.

Day 74 – 16ᵀᴴ September - Wells-next-the-Sea to Lowestoft

I had met our next companion, Roy Sherlock, at the Boat Show where he had expressed an interest in buying a Cape Cutter and he had sailed before on my

169

boat within the relatively sheltered waters of Chichester Harbour. He and his wife had met us the night we arrived so, when he realised Jilly was departing and there was room on the boat, he asked if he could accompany us on the next leg. This was his chance to see what a Cape Cutter could do in the open sea, and he strode down to the boat with some food and gear, keen to get going. Nothing quite like first-hand experience to find out what sailing a Cape Cutter is all about.

The trip south was a complete contrast to our last sailing experience, which was more likely to put anyone off going to sea at all, let alone invest in a boat. The winds were blowing from the right direction, the north-west at a moderate pace, the sea was big enough to be interesting, but certainly not rough, and together we had an enjoyable sail down around the Norfolk coast past the giant pier at Cromer and on to Lowestoft.

The port at Lowestoft is so busy that we had to wait for a traffic light system to indicate that we could enter the port. To this day I don't know what happened, maybe we were a bit slow or the other boat was anticipating the change, but as we went through the entrance after waiting for the lights to change in our favour, we almost collided with a pilot boat zooming out to sea. There was much yelling and shaking of fists, and luckily, while a close call, no contact was made. It certainly gave me one hell of a fright and it took some time to calm down. They do say that every day you should do something that scares you but some days on this trip I could seriously do without it!

Roy's wife and daughter Emily were at Lowestoft to meet us, along with Chal, my next crew member, and Sheila and Emily stayed to join us for supper at the Royal Norfolk Yacht Club before departing, with Roy, for their home back up the coast.

CHAPTER 21 – BLAST FROM THE PAST …

DAY 75 – 17TH SEPTEMBER - LOWESTOFT TO ORFORD

There was plenty of banter the next morning as David, Chal and I departed Lowestoft. Chal is a gaff rig sailor and grew up on the east coast so, at least after the bad experience with the local pilot the night before, I had my own local pilot on board. It is always so much more relaxing to sail with someone who knows the waters, knows the coast and knows how to sail a gaff rig. The trip was narrated with plenty of stories as we

Joined by Chaloner our local Pilot

sailed down past Southwold Pier and Aldeburgh and across Hollesley Bay to the entrance of the river Alde. We were making for Orford, an historical Suffolk town that was a major port in the middle ages, sitting on the coast where the rivers Alde and Ore met. With the natural movement of the silt and sand, Orford is now protected from the sea by a long sandbank that stretches down the coast to the river mouth. You pretty much have to sail past the town and then turn into the river and sail or in this case motor back up the river, with the sea on your right, literally just over the other side of the sandbank – in effect going back on yourself.

Up the River Alde at Orford

Hats off to the village of Orford … finest childhood memories

The constantly moving sands complicate the river entrance which, in theory, can only be negotiated in daylight as there's not much of a leading light and you have to see where you're going to cross the bar.

Orford was the home of my uncle Kenneth Sherlock, who was the vicar of Orford in the 1950s. I wanted to go and see the rectory as I used to go there as a small boy. I would escape my mum and go down to the water where I would sit

Orford's infamous Jolly Sailor Pub serving Adnams strong ale ...

on the little ferry boat that went across the water to the top secret communication station that used to be on the island.

We arrived at Orford Quay at about half past three and the small town was just as I remembered it, like something out of a quaint Victorian novel with untouched cobble lanes. We went ashore for a quick look at the rectory and then Chal told us of a wonderful local pub called The Jolly Sailor, which was built sometime in the late 16th or early 17th century supposedly from the timbers of a wrecked ship. In the past the pub had a reputation as a hangout for smugglers, which made it sound like a dodgy but interesting place to visit. He proceeded to herd us in that direction, in time for a late lunch. There he ordered three pints of Adnams, the local brew, which went down very well, but then he went on to order three more, and then three more.

Fortunately, by the time we had finished a wonderful meal of mashed potatoes with chicken and gravy, which soaked up some of the aftermath of our beverages, we were able to stagger back down towards the boat.

Down by the quay, we wandered past a couple of old fishermen who commented on our demeanour, "You look like you've had a good time." We stopped to talk to them and one of them asked, "What brings you to Orford?"

"Well," I said, "I've come to see where my uncle use to live."

*Orford Church where my Uncle Kenneth Sherlock was
Rector in 1950/60s*

Orford's famous medieval castle

"Oh aye, who's your uncle?"

"Kenneth Sherlock."

"Kenneth Sherlock!" piped up the other fisherman in a thick Suffolk accent, "I remember the Revd Kenneth Sherlock. He was a good man. He used to keep the rabbits down around these parts with his 4/10 shotgun."

Turns out that my uncle was a shooting vicar!

You don't meet many vicars that have a shotgun with intent …

We rowed back to the boat and Chal and I climbed nimbly aboard. David, with his shorter legs and arms, not to mention a few brews under his belt had a few attempts at climbing into the boat, succeeding at last with an undignified sort of half backwards tumble roll into the cockpit. Once we had all stopped laughing we settled down for a bit of a siesta and we all fell soundly asleep. Boy we must have been tired, I'm quite sure the amount of alcohol we consumed had nothing to do with it!

"I thought you were real sailors and could hold your ale," Chal said later quite non-plussed, when I commented on the effect of the beer.

"What were we drinking?" I asked.

"Adnams Super Strong Real Ale."

Probably about 5 or 6 per cent alcohol, which could explain a few things!

That night we couldn't be bothered going ashore, so I put on my chef's hat, figuratively speaking, and cooked a good wholesome dinner of … boiled eggs and soldiers – dippy eggs!

Up the River Deben, bound for Woodbridge   *Fund raising in action …*

DAY 76 – 18ᵀᴴ SEPTEMBER - ORFORD TO WOODBRIDGE

The next morning I wanted to visit the castle, built in the 12th century by Henry II, so I went ashore to climb the hill and explore. When I got back we headed back down the river to the sea and turned south towards our next destination, Woodbridge.

Many of the places we called in at were somewhat off the beaten track but Chal had said, "If I'm coming with you, you're going to explore my country!" I had therefore left the organisation of this leg of the voyage up to him.

We went into the river entrance at Felixstowe Ferry and then motor sailed a long way up the River Deben to Woodbridge. Chal had phoned the Commodore of the sailing club and he came down in his boat to meet us. He guided us back up the river and we tied up alongside the dock. The Deben Yacht Club is built on stilts and is the second oldest in England. Chal left us here but David and I stayed on and the Commodore very kindly gave us the keys to the clubrooms so we could make use of the showers and kitchen facilities.

That afternoon we saw two couples and their children watching us and they wandered down to talk to us, to find out what we were doing and asked if they could come aboard. We had a lovely afternoon chatting about our voyage and when they left one of the men put his hand in his pocket and gave us £20. I didn't even have to get out the lucky dip bag for the kids. The great thing about it was that, once he had given me £20, there was no way the other couple could leave without matching it. Fantastic!

DAY 77 – 19ᵀᴴ SEPTEMBER - WOODBRIDGE TO SHOTLEY

David made breakfast the next morning, making full use of the clubroom kitchen. We therefore had the full eggs and bacon, toast, marmalade and marmite breakfast before setting off for Shotley, where David was due to jump ship. Back down the river we went past lots of boats, birds and other gorgeous scenery. It really was a beautiful place and I can understand why Chal wanted to show it to us. We made our way carefully past Felixstowe Ferry and its adjacent sand bar and began to approach what is probably one of the busiest stretches of water in the whole of the UK, with lots of cross North Sea traffic coming in and out of the various ports in Harwich Harbour. Some of these ships are huge to look at from a distance so there was no way I wanted to get too close to them in my 19 foot boat. It would have been like looking up at a sky scraper. Not only would it block the wind and sun but, if I couldn't see the bridge of the ship, there was no way they could see me, a sure recipe for disaster. With this in mind we proceeded very cautiously indeed. Entering the waterway there, one can't help but be amazed at the vast expanse of container docks at the Port of Felixstowe on the east bank catering to the international sea freight industries. To the left, the area is fitted out to deal with the number of cross North Sea ferries that operate between Harwich, Europe and Scandinavia, carrying not only passengers but huge amounts of freight. We carried on past both of these busy commercial centres to the marina at Shotley, where I had been many times before during my numerous delivery voyages, and tied up alongside the dock. The marina lies at the end of an outcrop of land that divides the River Stour and the River Orwell. No sooner had we arrived than Maureen and John Whelton and Terri (Dave's wife, the Moore family ocean widow) met us and descended upon us for tea in the cockpit. Maureen and John, whom I knew from Royal Marine days later entertained David, Terri and I to a very slap up supper with lots of Royal Marine banter and 'trips down memory lane' in their Ipswich home. After supper, I bid farewell and returned to my ship as Terri had placed Dave firmly under house arrest. I needed to go so I could be ready for my next crew, who were due to arrive before the sparrows awoke, let alone thought of doing anything in the morning. I also wanted to have a very quick tidy of the boat before my new companions arrived.

DAY 78 – 20TH SEPTEMBER - SHOTLEY TO RAMSGATE

Bright and early the next morning, George Holroyd and Edward Johnson, Theo's dad and grandad, set out to meet me at Shotley Marina. Shotley is not particularly easy to find by road as it lies up what could be described as a middle finger of land and you have to drive quite some way through nothing but farmers' fields to get there. By the time they arrived, they were quite relieved as they felt they had been driving for ages and were getting nervous that they might be going the wrong way.

George was only with me for the day, while Edward was going to stay a bit longer. They stowed their gear and off we went, through the marina's lock and motor sailing back out past Harwich and down the coast.

It was a lovely day and they soon relaxed enough to enjoy themselves and forget, for just a little while, the stress they coped with on a normal day. Both of them lead very busy lives and were glad to sit back and have a relaxing sail. With their arrival, as if someone upstairs was making a point and, for one of the rare times in the whole trip, the wind swung round behind us and instead of being 'on da nose,' we had the wind 'on da bum!'

This area of the English coast is quite shallow and, as there are numerous rivers that make their way out to the sea, the water is often quite dirty looking with silt washed out of the estuaries. This in itself can make navigation difficult as the waves tend to stand higher when the seabed is shallow, objects are harder to see in the dirty water and you have to be careful not to get too close to shore as, particularly after a flood, sandbanks have a nasty habit of forming in places where they haven't done so before. This worsens the closer you get to the Thames Estuary, which spews out tonnes of mud each year.

We had to dodge through the sandbanks off the Thames Estuary, which fortunately are well marked, but you still need to keep your wits about you as not only do you have to avoid running aground, but avoid running into or being run over by one of the huge ships going in and out.

Feeling somewhat peckish, I peeked into the bag of goodies supplied by Eva (Edward's better half) to discover all my favourites … freshly baked crusty apple cake – a secret Swedish recipe – bacon and egg sandwiches, smoked salmon salad and ginger biscuits covered in thick dark chocolate (only from Waitrose!) What a floating feast we had and it's no wonder Edward has a constant smile on his face …

It was a lovely day of banter and stories. The two of them gave me a lot of ribbing about how much I had exaggerated about how bad the conditions had been, "Oh come on Mike," George said, "We know it's always like this! You've been pulling our legs!" They couldn't believe what I'd been through.

"It's a nice boat, it's sunny, it's warm, the wind's behind us so, what's the issue Mike? You've been telling fibs for the last three months!" they said.

"I have not been telling fibs!"

Of course I knew they were joking and joined in with the fun. We talked of all sorts of things, especially of Theo and the way the money I had raised might help him.

To have Theo's father, grandfather and godfather on the boat was absolutely magic. George and Edward had read all the blogs and followed the story of my journey and now, here they were, part of the story themselves. The flags and streamers were flying and we were sailing down the English coast, mile by mile getting closer to the end of the voyage. Fabulous stuff!

We got into Ramsgate and said goodbye to George who had to get back to London for work the next day. Ramsgate is a delightful town with a rich maritime heritage and some beautiful old buildings, fortunate to survive the bombings of the First and Second World Wars. Edward and I had a lovely supper in one of my favourite haunts: the loveliest fish 'n chip shop, run by a Turkish family. They had been there a long time and I often visited, when I was in Ramsgate on a boat delivery. There we were sitting beside the sea eating Turkish fish 'n chips in Ramsgate – how British!

CHAPTER 22 – ALMOST THERE …

DAY 79 – 21ST SEPTEMBER - RAMSGATE TO RYE

The tide was reasonably helpful so, after another, by now, famous Brookie's breakfast, we sailed out of Ramsgate, past the downs, round past the sea walls of Dover, checking on Channel 12 that we had permission from the harbour master to cross the ferry channel, and then proceeding, when they said *"Go"* with outboard motor at full revs charging forward into the English Channel.

On we sailed past Folkestone, now better known for its chunnel train crossing than the cross channel ferries it has hosted over the years, down past miles of sandy beaches, once so popular with British holiday makers and, now, largely deserted as people travel further afield to more tropical climates. We sailed past the dreaded low sandy headland of Dungeness. I say the dreaded headland of Dungeness not because it is now the site of a large nuclear power plant but rather because, over the years, it has caught out many a sailor who has run aground there in the fog. The entire English fleet of probably thirty sailing warships ended up there more than once. Sir Cloudesley Shovel was Admiral of the Fleet in the time of George II, sometime in the mid 1700s, and he kept putting the fleet onto the sands at Dungeness in the fog. This prompted the King to demand that someone solve the riddle of longitude so that his sailors could navigate accurately. Latitude was well known at the time and navigators could take a sighting at noon and work out how far off the horizon the sun had risen, which translated into how far north or south of the equator they were.

Longitude was far more complicated to work out and was finally solved when Harrison developed his various longitude chronometers. Basically he worked out that if you imagine the earth as an orange and cut it in half across the middle then each segment is one hour. So there are twenty four segments in the orange if it is to represent one day. Round the centre of a circle there are 360 degrees of arc, so each hour that the sun travels from east to west is equal to 15 degrees. Suddenly there was a relationship between time and arc so navigators were more accurately able to tell where they were. Not only could they give their position to the north and south, but also to the east and west. This at last put a stop to ships finding land when they did not intend to.

Harrison's clocks are in the Greenwich Meridian Museum – well worth a look if navigation 'lights your fire.'

Once round Dungeness, we sailed across the bay and into the narrow inlet of the River Rother, which is known to be extremely tidal. I'd never been anywhere near it before as I was usually sailing boats with long keels and anyone with a long keel beneath their hull does well to stay where the water is deep. In my little boat though, we were well suited to shallow water and we waited for the flood of the tide to help carry us up the river to Rye, where we had a lovely supper in the Union Inn, a pub I mention later as one of my top ten pubs in Britain. Hard to believe that Rye was once right on the coast but, having sailed past the many miles of sandy beaches and experienced the shifting sands off the east coast, it was easier to comprehend the powerful affect of nature on the landscape.

Edward was supposed to leave me at Rye but my next scheduled crew member was unable to make it so, with little persuasion from me, I managed to convince him to stay with me for one more day to Eastbourne.

DAY 80 – 22ND SEPTEMBER - RYE TO EASTBOURNE

Our luck with the weather continued and we had a wonderful day sailing with an easterly breeze pushing us from behind, calm seas and sunshine. Edward couldn't believe it and he commented as we sailed along, "Mike you've had a pub crawl around Britain in the sunshine!"

"Yes, I have," I said, "For the last two days out of eighty! Two eightieths whatever that is!"

We sailed on across Pevensey Bay and into the Sovereign Yacht Harbour at Eastbourne, another marina I was quite familiar with from my boat delivery trips. From Chichester Harbour you can make Eastbourne in a day, then a day to Dover, and then across the channel to the continent. I'm not the kind of delivery skipper that sails non-stop 24 hours a day, I like to do a long day and then pull into port for a night and have a pub supper and a good night's sleep before continuing, so Eastbourne had been a regular port of call.

Edward left me in Eastbourne, where I was not alone for long. David Moore, who had sailed with me on this adventure from Grimsby to Shotley, turned up to help me out for another day. His wife Terri dropped him off and arranged to pick him up again from Brighton the next night. He had teaching commitments but had squeezed me in to his busy schedule and was able to accompany me around Beachy Head.

Beachy Head is another one of those renowned sailing spots that, when it is good it is ever so good and when it is bad, it is horrid! I didn't really want to have to deal with it single handed in case the weather took a turn for the worse, so was very pleased and secretly relieved when David said he would sail with me for another day.

DAY 81 – 23ʀᴅ SEPTEMBER - EASTBOURNE TO BRIGHTON

Once again we set off in an easterly breeze and gorgeous sunshine and David too couldn't believe the weather but at least he knew how unusual it was and could appreciate it, unlike the last lot!

Beachy Head is a headland with sheer chalk cliff faces that are the highest in Britain, the highest rising to 530 feet or 162 metres above sea level. The peak allows views of the south east coast from Dungeness in the east, to Selsey Bill in the west. The name Beachy Head has nothing in fact to do with a beach and is rather a corruption of the original French words meaning "beautiful headland". It has been a landmark for sailors over the centuries, and is mentioned in one of my favourite sea shanties, so I have an unusual affinity with it.

At the base of the cliffs is of course a lighthouse, warning ships to keep well clear, and one can see why as it would be very hard to see the white of the cliffs in any kind of fog or bad weather, not to mention the incredible waves that nature must generate to wear away such magnificent walls, even if they are made of chalk.

On this particular occasion, the waters off Beachy Head behaved themselves, and without having to worry about ebbing tides, darkness or sick crew, David and I had a magnificent day's sailing around the not so foreboding headland and into Brighton Marina, which is one of a chain run by a company called Premier Marinas. Pete MacGregor, a good friend of mine and a highly qualified Health and Safety Officer who looks after Premier Marinas, told John Davey, the owner of the Brighton Marina, about us and John very generously put on a great welcome for us, providing us with a free berth and inviting us for lunch.

After lunch, Terri arrived to pick up David and take him away again to normality. Interesting to think that, at this stage of the voyage, my idea of normality was vastly different from theirs and I wondered how I would cope readjusting to what everyone else called normality on my return home.

I went back to the boat and, since I had a bit of time up my sleeve, fitted some preventers on the boom through snatch blocks. Preventers are designed to stop the boom from swinging wildly from one side to the other if the wind changes suddenly without warning or if you accidentally crash jibe. A bit late you might say and I would have to agree. They should probably have gone on much earlier than Day 81 of 86, especially since I had carried them virtually all the way round Britain but had never got round to fitting them till now. What is it they say about an ounce of prevention?

I might point out that you don't really need preventers when the wind is on the nose, which seemed to be the situation for most of the trip, but no excuses really. Now I was to sail on my own for a day and, since I had the time, it was now prudent to set the boat up as best I could for all eventualities.

Among my other confessions, I must admit to the gaps in my log book, which I'm ashamed of, and the bits of kit that didn't get screwed on but my daily priority of survival didn't always get as far as the niceties of such things. I did enough to get by. Captain James Cook probably wouldn't be proud of me but one is never perfect and there's always room for improvement, if one has the energy and time. It just so happened that, for once, on Day 82 of my voyage, I actually had both the energy and the time.

DAY 82 – 24ᵀᴴ SEPTEMBER - BRIGHTON TO LITTLEHAMPTON

I sailed away the next morning past the many big hotels and buildings that line Brighton Beach, past the pier with its roller coaster and funfair rides and past the burnt out structure of the old pier that still stands just off the shore, cut off from the beach as if waiting for something.

I was all on my own. It was nice. I had another beautiful day, it was sunny, the wind was from the east blowing me along from behind, there were no big bits of rock or land sticking out, favourable tide and I had my preventers. What else could I ask for?

I sailed almost due west passing West Pier at Worthing and continuing along the shoreline as if tracking the cars and trucks that sped along the coastal road.

Ahead of me I could see Selsey Bill, the last headland before home, and with a sense of anticipation I turned towards the entrance of the Arun River and motored into Littlehampton, where, for only the third time in my entire journey, I had to pay berthing fees. Another council run wharf and no leeway. Rules are rules and the miserable bloke wasn't interested in hearing my story.

Entering Littlehampton after a solo leg from Brighton

Littlehampton is close to East Preston, where David Moore and his wife Terri live, so they came down that afternoon, fished me off the boat, took me back to their house and basically put me in the bath for two days.

"You need a bath," Terri said, "Your clothes are atrocious. Your body is heaving. You stink and you smell. Your hair is far too long. You are nothing more than a cave man pretending to be a yachtsman. We're going to use the next two days to get you clean and fit to be seen in public." So they did. I even got to sleep in a real bed for a night once I dragged myself once more from a cold bath after falling asleep for the fourth time in my journey while soaking.

Day 83 & 84 – 25th & 26th September – Littlehampton

I had two days off, partly because I had got ahead of myself with the lovely easterly breeze, and also because I wanted James and Jayne, my son and daughter-in-law to accompany me on the last leg home to Bosham. They were working and couldn't get off work until the Friday night and my arrival at Bosham Quay was timed for noon on Sunday.

Day 85 – 27th September - Littlehampton to Hayling Island

On the morning of the 27th James and Jayne were delivered to the boat by my lovely Pippa; I was so glad to see again as talking on the phone was not the same as being with someone. We all had breakfast on the quayside at the Bellaton Restaurant (since closed), where George gave us free coffees and was a very pleasant host.

I was praying right up until that morning that the lovely weather would continue, and was extremely glad when the sun continued to shine and the wind continued to blow from the east. Jayne confessed to me, as we set off, that she was feeling a little queasy, and I was delighted when she added the real reason … that she was two months pregnant with my second grandchild! She was so keen to continue, despite feeling ill, and, as the conditions were mild, I was hopeful she would be able to last the distance to Hayling Island without being sick. Her first son Jack was only 17 months old at the time and, as we had to sail around Selsey Bill, a large headland which needs careful negotiation, we thought it better that he stayed with Pippa.

James, Jayne and Jack last leg crew mates

We had a marvellous sail, talking non-stop about the trip. We were going along with the tide, with the wind behind us, chatting away, when out of the corner of my eye I saw a channel marker. The only problem, was that the channel marker was on the wrong side of the boat!

Off Selsey Bill there's a marker that you have to go outside in order to get into the Looe Channel, a very narrow channel between two buoys known as Street and Boulder, green and red. I was on the inside of the marker, and as all sailors know, a marker is usually there for a very good reason, so whatever that reason was, was good enough for me.

As calmly as possible, I quickly pretended that all was well as I pulled in the gennaker, rounded up the boat, started the engine and motored back over to the marker and around the right side. Phew!

It was just another reminder that poor seamanship can bite you on the bum without a moment's notice. You have to be on the ball constantly. One can never allow oneself to get distracted at sea, for that one moment's lack of concentration can mean the difference between safety and disaster.

We sailed across the bay to Chichester Harbour and, as we approached the harbour, I saw a little boat sitting at the harbour entrance. My neighbour, Peter Trewill, and his co-owner, Simon Hoy, had come out in their Cornish Shrimper *Jenessa* to meet us. I was really chuffed. It was great to have a welcoming party. What a lovely thing to do. Good men!

We got safely into Sparkes Marina on Hayling Island without a hitch, tying up at the dock in conditions that were in stark contrast to those I had left in eighty odd days before. No rolling waves, no howling gales and no pouring rain. What a difference!

Pippa joined us and dinner at the marina restaurant, Marina Jacks, was fabulous that night. We had a celebratory supper with lobster and champagne. Jayne went back to Bosham with Pippa that evening to tend to Jack, but James stayed with me on the boat to help me prepare her for the grand homecoming at Bosham Quay the next day.

Me and my boat ...

CHAPTER 23 – GOING HOME

Day 86 – 28th September - Hayling Island to Bosham

James and I got up early that Sunday morning and dressed the boat in all her finery. Flags, streamers, and bunting, what a sight! Jayne rejoined us with little Jack, complete with a baby lifejacket, and we set off up the harbour past East Head, Itchenor and Cobnor, where there was a huge cheer (thanks Bosham Sailing Club and the 420 class sailors!) and, give or take a few seconds at midday, we reached Bosham Quay. Jayne steered the boat into the quay, our lines were taken and I leapt ashore hat in one hand, foghorn in the other, to be met by Pippa holding an ice cold bottle of Moet in her hands which was duly sprayed, Lewis Hamilton style, over anyone in range before I downed the rest and shook a forest of hands … I had finally made it back to where I had started. Gone was the stormy weather, replaced by lovely sunshine. Well, that was my Grand Prix moment! It was a bit of a shame to waste a good bottle of champagne but how often do you celebrate something like that?

What a crowd had turned out to meet us; there were family, people from the village, Fight for Sight workers, clergy, yacht club members, the press …

It was an amazing feeling. I was just, sort of floating. It all happened around me, people looking after the boat, people talking, taking pictures. Even Admiral Sandy Woodward was there. He had sent us off and was there again to welcome us back. It was all a bit much really and I was elated but mentally and physically exhausted.

Pip had organised a lunch at the sailing club so we all adjourned back there for speeches and food. There was even a *Theo's Future* cake that looked just like *Sea Badger II*, which Pip had obviously spent a lot of time making. Well done her!

Like my send off, everyone wanted to say something to welcome me back. I thanked everyone profusely for their

Pippa's creation - a representation of Theo's Future in cake!

Steady as she goes!

Approaching Bosham Quay, wow – can't quite believe it – 200 metres to go!

Nearly there after 86 days at sea

Leap of faith …

… into Pippa's arms

Only Moet will do … Good enough for Napoleon – certainly good enough for me!

support and found it hard to believe that the project I had put so much energy into for so long was actually over. It started to dawn on me that this was it. I was back. I had done it.

At last the party was concluded, the crowds started to disperse and normality, whatever that was, to a certain extent, returned. We went to move the boat to her normal mooring and, while we were out on the water, the local GP Michael Gilbert and his wife, who were out in their canoes came alongside. He took my line and clipped it on to the mooring for me. "How are you Mike?" he asked, "You didn't have the services of your GP on the way round."

"Ahh," I said, "No Michael, but when you go to sea, provided you take your fruit juice, it's a healthy environment." (Apart from the odd mishap like the splinter in my foot but I wasn't going to tell him about that.)

"Very pleased to hear it," he said, and produced a bottle of champagne for me. How nice!

When we got back to the house, I gave some more interviews with the local press, had my photo taken a few more times and, finally, once the press had left, and there was no one to impress, I basically collapsed. Not physically, but inside I suddenly felt completely drained. The adrenaline rush of arriving back was fading away and I suddenly realised that yes, I had done it; I had achieved what I set out to do. It was over. So what? It was extraordinary really. I had such mixed emotions of achieving my goal. What on earth was I supposed to do now?

Next day, I couldn't even bring myself to go out to the boat. It had been my home for so long and yet now I couldn't face it. It took several days before I could even bring myself to go and check that everything on board was sorted. I had no desire to spend any time on board and felt quite apathetic, even about organising to get her out of the water and preparing her for the winter ahead.

I know now that life for me became a bit of a struggle for a while …

It is by no means an excuse but I think, if you read stories of mariners and explorers, you find out that, when they come home, they have a phase of real downturn, having extended themselves, riding on the top of a psychological wave and then falling into a kind of depression and, as I know, the reciprocal trough can be very deep indeed.

I felt very low for quite some time.

"Right Mike," said Chal enthusiastically one day, "I'll help you write the book now."

"No Chal, I can't. I'm not even sure that there will be a book. I don't even want to think about it." was my reply.

"Oh" he said, unsure what to say or do next I imagine.

I felt that people wanted me to be more than myself and I didn't have the capacity. My batteries were completely flat. Pip reckoned I'd strained

From L to R Michelle Action CX Fight for Sight, Dr Ulrich Luhmann, Dr Viet Tran, Mike Brooke, Jayne hold Jack, James, Pippa, Chaloner, Mary, Claire and Sal

myself mentally and physically and it took a good six months for me to be my normal self again.

The truth was, though, regardless of the aftermath, my depression or anything else, I had done it.

I had set out to sail around Britain and raise £27,000 and I had. In fact the target amount was achieved when I was still on my way and I'm pleased to say that when all the donations were tallied up the total by the time I reached Bosham was £33,500.

Further funds have continued to arrive in bits and pieces, as a result of other fundraising that went on, and the total is now well over £43,000!

So really, was it worth it …

Yes!

Back on her mooring after 1783 nautical miles

EPILOGUE

There are many who would say I am mad, and, in fact, some who have said this to my face – usually after spending some time aboard with me on my voyage. While many have sailed around the UK before, few have set themselves such an arduous task in such a small boat. There were times when I was worried we may not make it, that I had bitten off more than I could chew, and that my boat and I were not up to the task ahead.

Some things I'm afraid had to take less importance. Keeping the log up to date was something I tried to do but found myself falling further behind on a daily basis. You arrive in a new port, tired, hungry, thirsty, and sometimes wet. There's no chart table in the boat, no room to spread out papers. To be honest, you're in a glorified dinghy. The log at times was a little neglected, but I had my tracker working which recorded my speed and direction, I was writing my blog for the website so, at times, that had to do.

I think, quite frankly, that I overdid it. I was sailing six or seven hours nearly every day on a tidal gate. I'd leave my anchorage or berth when the tide was favourable, sometimes at five or six in the morning, stay at sea for six or seven hours until the tide turned and was unfavourable, and then make it to a port or bay for the night, hopefully without losing too much ground by slipping backward on the opposing tide. Most evenings I'd have to negotiate a channel, bay or harbour entrance and then pick up a mooring, set the anchor or tie up in a berth. Once the boat was stationary I'd have to make sure everything was tidy and ready for the next day, fix anything that needed mending, and work out what we needed ashore.

I was not only getting the boat from A to B, but facing the pub experience in the evening. Yes, it's great to have a beer. Yes, you have to get some grub. My body was saying, "Go to bed," but my heart was saying, "We have to raise the money for the scanner." So, I'd take a big breath, remember what I was doing this for and rally the troops for the trip ashore, which on a good night meant simply stepping onto the dock, but at other times rowing ashore.

The trick was to get to shore before the whole town shut for the night, do what shopping was needed, then find a pub and organise to set up my stand and start fundraising, which required an effort all of its own.

You can't just beg, you can't just stand there. You have to work the room, repeating your story, answering questions, listening to others and comparing adventures. People have got to believe in what you're doing and feel that your personal endeavour is worth them putting their hand in their pocket and donating their £5 note.

It didn't pay to stop and think about how far I still had to go on my voyage. I had to work at times on a day-by-day basis and, if that got too much, hour-by-hour or minute-by-minute. My own morale was crucial as I knew I was less effective and possibly more dangerous, when my spirits were low and I allowed my judgment and decision making to be clouded by other worries.

I was fortunate indeed to have such marvellous companions on my journey, without whom I wouldn't have been able to complete my task. This man is not meant to be a solo animal and, while many take on far greater voyages on their own than I, and I take my hat off to them, I have come to recognise the need I personally have for support, conversation, teamwork and a shared joke. After all, a sea shanty always sounds best when sung by a raucous crew. Perhaps it is a throwback to my heritage and military lifestyle but I have always believed the whole is greater than the sum of the individuals. This journey, a journey of hope, endeavour and, indeed, a journey of personal discovery, was very much a team effort as I would not have been able to make it on my own.

When I started this journey, I had every faith in my ability as a sailor, as a skipper and navigator, and felt that the vessel I had chosen was up to the mark. For the first time, perhaps, as Dick Pratt and I struggled hour after hour to make headway through those treacherous seas along the southern coast, it dawned on me that I had launched myself once more into a project that, while sounding exciting and attainable in theory, in reality was to take its toll on me, both physically and mentally. On reflection afterwards, there were times when I had to dig deep and put my trust not only in my sailing companions but in complete strangers and, on many occasions, in some higher being to help me through when times were tough.

On my return, I gave thanks to the Good Lord in my local church at Bosham. My sister, Mary, told me on my return that, on the Sunday after I left at the very start of my voyage, the vicar Canon Tom Inman got the entire congregation to stop and think of me, at sea, and to join him in a prayer for my safe return. How lovely to be part of such a community and in fact to discover the kindness of Britain's larger community on my voyage.

Success for me was on several levels. Yes, I had successfully negotiated my way round the country in a little boat. Yes, I had raised more money than the sum needed. Yes, I managed to get all my crew safely round. And yes, the boat had been up to the job. In some ways for me the greatest success was not so much a tangible thing but, rather, a renewed faith in life. A belief that there is a plan. That the Lord does work in mysterious ways and that I have, in some small and humble way, served humanity on Simon's behalf.

'Big Man'
(a tribute to Simon Brooke by his father)

Big Man, he's in Heaven!
Yes, he's there for sure.
Big Man, he's in Heaven!
He passed through that door.

Where is Heaven, we don't know,
it's so hard to bear.
Where is Heaven, we don' t know,
but, for sure, he's there.

He would not want us to grieve
for him for too long.
He would want us to march forward,
with a happy song!

Where is Heaven, we don't know,
it's so hard to bear.
Where is Heaven, we don't know,
but, for sure, he's there.

Mike Brooke

ACKNOWLEDGEMENTS

There are so many people who I need to thank. Some have been paramount in making sure I achieved my goal. Others played a smaller part but, without it, I may not have been able to succeed. Many do not even know that they played a part at all in my success but I am grateful to all who helped me in some way, especially the Good Lord who often had to step up to the plate to make sure I was safe.

Thanks first to my darling wife Pip, who kept the home fires burning while I was away. She had perhaps the longest job and carried the largest burden. Not only did she have to put up with me through the planning process, keep things going on her own while I was away, but also deal with what was left of me when I got back, and I know that was not easy.

To my eldest son, Simon, whom I thought of often in my voyage and who, I am sure, would be pleased with my efforts.

To his younger brother, James, and daughter-in-law Jayne, who have supported the old man in another hare-brained scheme and, like Pip, have been involved since the beginning when the reality of the journey was only an idea.

To George and Elin who opened their hearts to me, accepted me as their child's godfather on Simon's behalf and got me started on this journey in the first place.

To my godson, Theo, who became the face of the campaign and is such a lovely wee chap who deserves the best that life and I can give him.

To my family, my brother, Johnny, who oversaw the starting ceremony, my sister-in-law, Jane, who made sure the Good Lord kept an eye on me in my travels, and sister, Mary, who took the time to be part of the story.

To Chal Chute, my self-appointed guru, who guided me through a minefield of 'this and that' to get started and then tracked my progress and coordinated my journey round the coast, communicating with the many ports and harbours I visited so they knew to expect me.

To Nick Sherman who set up and kept my web page alive and, like many others, was part of the journey.

To Michele Acton from Fight for Sight without whose practical contribution and support we could never have undertaken this project.

To Admiral Sandy Woodward for his encouragement, wisdom and for writing the Foreword.

To Dean Nicholas who forsook the Cathedral Cloisters to be amongst us all and lead the blessing and naming ceremony at the start with Revd Jane, soaking us in holy water!

To Canon Tom Inman who, at the start, reminded us of Sir Francis Drake's immortal words, "The job isn't done 'til it's thoroughly finished!" No pressure, Mike, I could hear him thinking at the time …

To Professor Moore, who has made so much progress in developing new ways to help blind people, especially the children like little Theo.

To my sailing companions and their families, who let them loose to sail with me; Nick Sherman, Dick Pratt, Lieutenant Colonel Pat Clarke, Jilly Rumble, Claire Hall, Oscar Nowak, Mary Brooke, Daisy Wylam, David Pratt, Robert Goodall, Pip, Georgina Peters, Laura Fulton, Colonel Tim Weeks OBE, Anna Woods, Jane Turner, Major Richard Peters, David Moore, Roy Sherlock, Chal Chute, George Holroyd, Edward Johnson, James, Jayne and Jack Brooke.

The many who sponsored me by donating goods, time and materials, or perhaps eased the prices of things I needed for the trip;

Bob and Norma Brown from Honnor Marine, David Pougher and his PA Linda of Yamaha UK, Christian Brewer from Barton Maine, Stuart Anderson from SeaTeach Marine, John Bland from TecSew in Gosport for their amazing canvas work, Mark Trevatt of Horizon Soft Furnishings who upgraded the bunk cushions, Honda UK, Craft Insure, Supersigns, Lester Abbott and Clare Horsman of Southerley Yachts for marketing, Made to Measure Fenders for customised fendering, TrackTrans Trackers who monitored my progress round Britain and, of course, Hyde Sails. Then there were Nigel and Kay Glennie of Whacky Practicals on their sons, tom and Jamie.

To Dame Ellen MacArthur, Sir Robin Knox-Johnson and Captain James Cook who were, at times, my inspiration.

To the many others who met me, fed me, washed my clothes, cheered me up, shared a meal, gave me free berthing, opened their homes, gave me a bath, shared their sailing clubs, gave me a lift in their car, fixed my boat, helped me with directions, lent me a mooring for the night without even knowing about it, made me laugh, shared a story, or kept their pub open just a little past closing time so we could get a much needed refreshing pint and in some way made my journey all the richer. There are many named below and probably just as many I never knew by name, but my thanks goes out to them all the same:

Prof Tony Moore with Michele Acton expressing huge thanks to everyone who had worked so hard to raise the money for the scanner

Simon Veysey, Mike McGrail, Diana Chute, Rosie Sherman, Gavin King, The Yarmouth Harbour Master who shared his tucker, Caroline and Tim Harding, Mark and Alison Tilley, The Royal Artillery crew at the Bovington Tank Firing Range who stopped shooting at us, Colonel Michael Gill MBE, Neil the Brixton Harbour Master, Judi Hedger, Claire Hall, her husband Simon and lovely daughters Georgia and Olivia, Teresa and Jay, my niece Janey and her son Freddie, Chris Hoyle of Hoyle Marine, Stephanie Clark, The Helicopter crew at Royal Navy Air Station Culdrose, Sir Turtle of the Cayman Islands, Gary Aston of Marine-Tech in St Ives, Rick Stein's Café, Padstow Sailing Club, Will and Helen Shingler of the Grosvenor Hotel at Bude, the two doctors, their wives and fifteen children on Lundy Island, King Neptune, the Dale Sailing Club, Geoff and Sarah Browning, John, Fred, Gwynn, John and Dick from Neyland Sailing Club, Frank Penfold, Bill the Harbour Master at Aberaeron, Nick and Liz, Keith and Bob, Briony and Stuart at the Tycock Inn in Porth Dinllaen, Geoff Garrard at Holyhead Marina, Suzanne, Gweneth, Ruth and Jamie, Peggy at the Holyhead Yacht Club, Pat and his daughter Hannah, Simon Tuck at the Albert Pub at Port St Mary who did the hard work fundraising and dared me to bare my bottom, James from Douglas, Eric the Harbour Master at Douglas, Janine from 'Pure Inspiration', David and Diana at the Crown Hotel, Glenn who captured the frivolity, the lifeboat crew at Port Patrick, Kate, Richard, Finley and Imogen Moody at Crinan, Jim Shearer, Lochaber Yacht Club at Fort William, the Lock Keeper at Corpach, Stuart Leitch and Frances from The Moorings Hotel at Banavie, Carol and Colin Gilmour, Scott Anderson at Cayley Marina, Sqn Ldr Nigel Hessing and his crew on RAF yacht *Driftwood*, Tim McKeown, Dr Kevin Robinson, Jim the Marina Manager at Peterhead, the staff

A sense of great relief as I finally cut the ribbon

at Royal Quays Marina in Tynemouth, the Harbour Master and his monkey at Hartlepool, Glen from Whitby Lifeboat, Steve, Scarborough Sailing Club, Humber Cruising Club, Grimsby Sailing Club, Sid at Grimsby, John Harrison who sorted out the longitude mess, Pete MacGregor, John Davey from Brighton Marina, Terri Moore, Bellaton Restaurant, Paul from Sparkes Marina, Simon from 'Marina Jacks', Nick Hayes, the entire Bosham community, who showed their support for my venture.

Last but not least, a huge and heart-felt thank you to Colonel Nigel Montagu and Jacqui Thorndick of the Institution of Royal Engineers together with graphic designer, Fernando Venzano, without whose patience, help and professional advice this book could simply not have been published.

Finally, thanks to the many who made donations along the way, contributing to the success of my mission.

"How exciting is that!"

One last thought –

"When you're sailing you're living …
Everything else is just waiting!"

Theo's Future on her moorings at Bosham - home again
©2013 Chris Hatton by kind permission
www.chrishattonphotography.com

THE CAPE CUTTER SPECIFICATIONS:

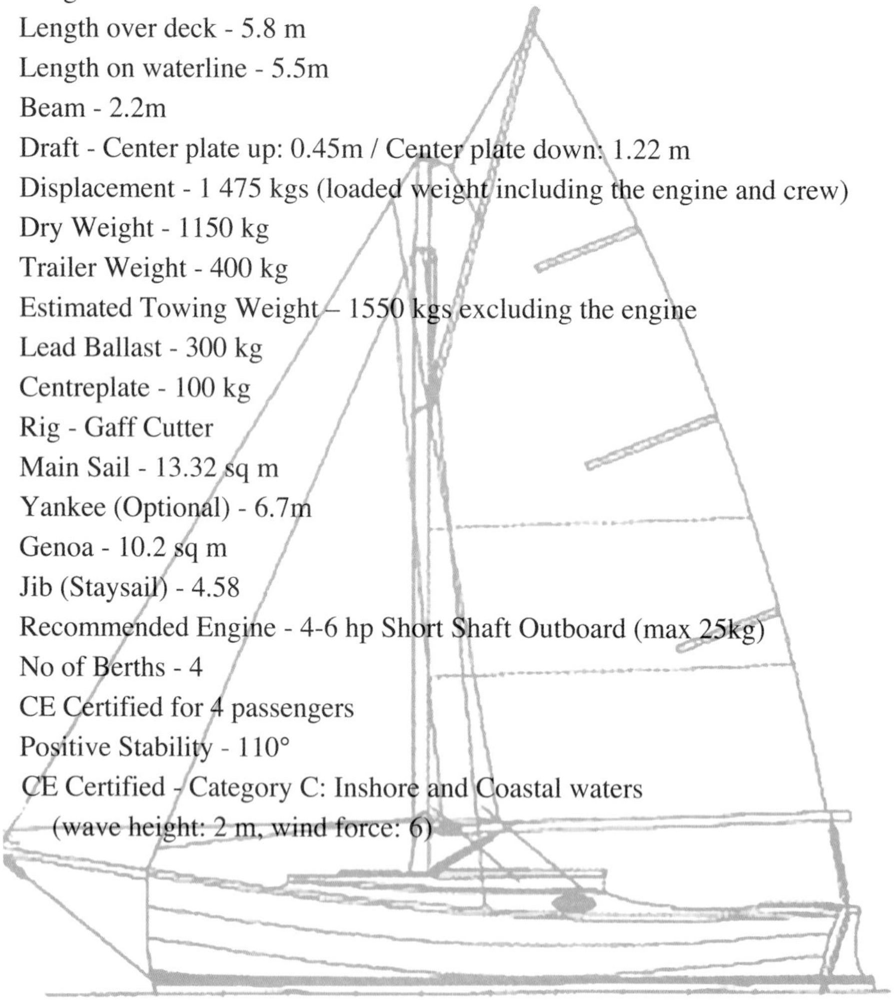

Designer - Dudley Dix

Length overall - 7.2 m

Length over deck - 5.8 m

Length on waterline - 5.5m

Beam - 2.2m

Draft - Center plate up: 0.45m / Center plate down: 1.22 m

Displacement - 1 475 kgs (loaded weight including the engine and crew)

Dry Weight - 1150 kg

Trailer Weight - 400 kg

Estimated Towing Weight – 1550 kgs excluding the engine

Lead Ballast - 300 kg

Centreplate - 100 kg

Rig - Gaff Cutter

Main Sail - 13.32 sq m

Yankee (Optional) - 6.7m

Genoa - 10.2 sq m

Jib (Staysail) - 4.58

Recommended Engine - 4-6 hp Short Shaft Outboard (max 25kg)

No of Berths - 4

CE Certified for 4 passengers

Positive Stability - 110°

CE Certified - Category C: Inshore and Coastal waters

(wave height: 2 m, wind force: 6)

INTERESTING FACTS

- 1783 nautical miles sailed with the wind 'on de nose' for 11 out of 12 weeks!
- 60 ports visited: 31(England); 10(Wales); 15(Scotland); 3(IoM); 1(NI).
- Over £43,000 raised at time of going to print and still going up.
- 25 different crew members from 18 months to 68 years old!
- Largest pod of dolphins – at least 30, all munching spawning salmon at the mouth of the River Tay near Dundee.
- Longest daily run 12.5 hours – 59nm from Grimsby to Wells-next-the-Sea.
- Historical Places of Interest visited:
  Captain Scott Antarctic Museum/RRS Discovery in Dundee
  Nelson's last surviving frigate - HMS Trincomalee - at Hartlepool
  Captain Cook Museum and treasures in Whitby
- Fuel consumed – approx 520 litres of petrol.
- Most people onboard – 21 for 'sundowners' in Lundy (6 adults and 15 children) – the self-draining cockpit was half full of water!!
- Top 12 pubs/eating establishments (in order of attendance):
  Cherub – Dartmouth (E)
  Admiral Benbow – Penzance (E)
  Rick Stein's Fish 'n Chips – Padstow (E)
  Ty Coch Inn – Porthdinllaen (W)
  Mount Stewart Hotel – Portpatrick (S)
  Londonderry Arms – Carnlough (NI)
  Moorings Hotel – Benavie, Caledonian Canal (S)
  Leon's Fish Restaurant – Grimsby (E)
  Jolly Sailor – Orford (E)
  Union Inn – Rye (E)
  Balaton Café – Littlehampton (E) sadly since closed.
  Marina Jacks – Sparkes Marina, Hayling Island (E)

Schedule and Crew List

Leg	From	To	Start	Finish	Via	Crew 1	Crew 2
1	5-Jul	11-Jul	Bosham	Brixham	Yarmouth	Dick Pratt	Nick Sharman
					Poole	Dick Pratt	
					Weymouth	Patrick Clarke	
2	12-Jul	18-Jul	Brixham	Padstow	Dartmouth	Patrick Clarke	Jilly Rumble
					Salcombe	Patrick Clarke	Jilly Rumble
					Falmouth	Patrick Clarke	Jilly Rumble
					Penzance	Patrick Clarke	Claire Horn
					St Ives	Patrick Clarke	
3	19-Jul	25-Jul	Padstow	Milford-Haven	Bude	Oscar Nowak	
					Lundy	Oscar Nowak	
					Tenby	Oscar Nowak	Mary Brooke
					Neyland	Oscar Nowak	Mary Brooke
4	26-Jul	1-Aug	Milford	Holyhead	Fishguard	Oscar Nowak	Daisy Wylam
					Pwllheli	Oscar Nowak	Daisy Wylam
					Porthe Dwil-laen	Oscar Nowak	Daisy Wylam
5	2-Aug	8-Aug	Holyhead	Port Patrick	Port St Mary	David Pratt	
					Douglas	David Pratt	
					Ramsey	David Pratt	
6	9-Aug	15-Aug	Port Patrick	Fort William	Carnlough	Robert Goodall	David Pratt
					Port Ellen	Robert Goodal	David Pratt
					Crinnan	Robert Goodall	David Pratt
					Oban	Robert Goodall	David Pratt
7	16-Aug	22-Aug	Fort William	Inverness	Gairlochy	Pippa Brooke	
					Fort Augustus	Pippa Brooke	
					Lewiston	Pippa Brooke	

Schedule and Crew List

Leg	From	To	Start	Finish	Via	Crew 1	Crew 2
8	23-Aug	29-Aug	Inverness	Dundee (Tayport)	Lossiemouth	Georgina Peters	Laura Fulton
					Gardenstown	Georgina Peters	Laura Fulton
					Peterhead	Georgina Peters	Laura Fulton
					Stonehaven	Georgina Peters	Laura Fulton
9	30-Aug	5-Sep	Dundee (Tayport)	Newcastle	Anstruther	Tim Weeks	Anna Woods and Jane Turner
					Eyemouth	Tim Weeks	
					Holy Island	Tim Weeks	
10	6-Sep	12-Sep	Tynemouth (Newcastle)	Grimsby	Hartlepool	Richard Peters	
					Whitby	Richard Peters	
					Scarborough	Richard Peters	
					Bridlington	Richard Peters	
11	13-Sep	19-Sep	Grimsby	Harwich (Shotley)	Wells-next-the-Sea	David Moore	Jilly Rumble
					Lowestoft	David Moore	Chal Chute
					Orford	David Moore	Chal Chute
					Woodbridge	David Moore	Chal Chute
12	20-Sep	28-Sep	Harwich (Shotley)	Bosham	Ramsgate	Edward Johnson	George Holroyd
					Rye	Edward Johnson	
					Eastbourne	Edward Johnson	
					Brighton	David Moore	
					Littelhampton	Solo	
					Hayling Is	James Brooke	Jayne Brooke
					Bosham	James Brooke	Jayne Brooke Jack Brooke

SIMON BROOKE - Remembered by his Friends ...

Simon Brooke died on 24 August 2003. He is a man to remember. He enlivened our lives with his good humour, and was a great friend and competitor. In quieter moments, I raise my thoughts to a particular mountain view - to remember him, and to remember what life means.

Photo of Simon Brooke ©2003 Ray Pritchard, by kind permission. Photo-montage from an idea by Dave Cuthill by Bev Kelly. Both Ray and Dave were skiing friends and colleagues.

Dear Reader,

Thank you for purchasing this little book about a big journey, which Dads undertook to raise funds for eyesight research. Please rest assured that every penny raised from the sale of this book will go towards Fight for Sight and the Cetacean Research and Rescue Unit, researching into and rescuing sea mammals, which was very close to Simon's heart. Both are amazing charities and doing wonderful work.